CAT SHOWS

- AND SUCCESSFUL SHOWING -

CAT SHOWS

- AND SUCCESSFUL SHOWING -

GRACE POND & MARY DUNNILL

BLANDFORD PRESS
POOLE · DORSET

First published in the UK 1985 by Blandford Press,
Link House, West Street, Poole, Dorset, BH15 1LL

Distributed in the United States by
Sterling Publishing Co., Inc.,
2 Park Avenue, New York, N.Y. 10016

British Library Cataloguing in Publication Data

Pond, Grace
  Cat shows and successful showing.
  1. Cats—Showing
  I. Title   II. Dunnill, Mary
  636.8'0888   SF445

  ISBN 0 7137 1373 9

Typeset by August Filmsetting, Haydock, St. Helens
Printed and bound in Great Britain by
Purnell & Sons Ltd, Paulton, Somerset

Contents

Acknowledgements

The authors would like to express their thanks and appreciation for the hours Miss Mary Hodgkinson spent going through old copies of *Fur and Feather* seeking out useful information, to Mrs Linda Emery of South Africa, Mrs Edna Field of Canada, and Mrs Lesley Morgan, of Tasmania, Australia for the up-to-date information on the Cat Fancy in their countries; to Mrs Marna Fogarty, Editor of the C.F.A. Year Book for her help in supplying addresses, and to the various fanciers in Britain that wrote regarding old books and early cat shows. Marc Henrie deserves a special vote of thanks for the hours he spent seeking out and photographing the beautiful cats and kittens depicted in this book.

Colour plates 14 and 15 are reproduced by kind permission of Spectrum Colour Library.

1 History of the Domestic Cat

Fifty million years ago there was a small and primitive mammal called *Miacis*; he had a long body and long tail, his legs were short and he looked like a weasel. From *Miacis* came the carnivores: the cat family, the dogs, bears, racoons and hyenas. The first cat, *Dinictis*, was about the size of a lynx, and his descendants developed in two directions: firstly, the sabre-toothed cats (*Smilodon*); and secondly the canine-toothed cats (the civet, the genet, the mongoose and the family Felidae to which all cats, domestic and wild, belong).

Millions of years before the beginning of historic times, the felids were spread around the earth, adapting to a wide range of environments. Some, for example the sabre-tooths, became extinct. By the time of the great ice ages, when primitive man was well established, the felids were similar to those of today, but greater in variety. In the aeons of development from *Dinictis*, there have evolved innumerable variations in size, shape, markings and habits. The basic characteristics, however, remain the same, and all cats are by instinct hunters and killers, whether they are solitary animals or live in groups.

There are now two main genera of cats: *Panthera*, which comprises lions, leopards, jaguars, panthers, pumas and ocelots; and *Felis*, which includes all the smaller cats. The cheetah and lynx are given genera of their own. *Felis* has four species: *F. sylvestris* (the European Wild Cat), *F. libyca* (the African Wild Cat), *F. manul* (Pallas' Cat), a native of Mongolia, and *F. catus*, the domestic cat, which is commonly thought to have descended from the African Wild Cat. How domestication actually occurred, however, is a matter for theory rather than fact.

Between prehistoric and historic times there is little known about the cat. Man and dog probably joined forces about ten thousand years ago but it may have been several thousand years afterwards that the cat came in from the cold. There are myths and legends to explain the domestication of the cat but little true evidence. One legend comes from old India: 'There was a time when the cat lived with the tiger, her brother. He grew sick and began to shiver and she knew that she must find fire to warm him. But only man had fire. When she reached his house to ask for some there was no-one there. She went in to take some fire but before she reached it she saw some tasty fish and some delicious rice on the floor. Unable to resist such a feast she helped herself and was just about to curl up for an after-dinner nap in front of the fire when she remembered why she had come. She took a burning brand between her teeth and ran back to her brother but, as soon as she had kindled a fire to warm him, she announced that she had found a new way of life and was going to live with man where there was good food for the taking and it was always warm.'

It has never been established whether man captured the cat or was adopted by it. The first stages in the domestication of the cat are to be found about 45,000 years ago in Ancient Egypt, along the Upper Nile. Although it is generally believed that the Kaffir cat, *Felis libyca*, from the North African desert, is an ancestor of our domestic cat, it is probably not the only one. There are claims that cats were kept in the Near East much earlier than in Egypt but most of our knowledge comes from Ancient Egypt.

Paintings and inscriptions from 2000 BC and thereafter give evidence that the Egyptians kept cats. The early presence of the domestic cat has been established in India, and Chinese literature of about 800 BC mentions the house cat. There is little evidence of the domestic cat in Ancient Greece, but slowly the custom of keeping cats spread. At an early date the cat was established in Syria. The Arabs kept cats in the sixth century. The Romans introduced them throughout their Empire, in every corner of Europe, even Britain, in the tenth century. Much later European explorers, colonisers and traders took cats to all parts of the world.

Over the centuries, the domestic cat has been venerated as a god, tortured as a devil, persecuted as a familiar of witches, praised in literature, represented in art, pampered by nobility, companion and friend to many, and a valuable commodity as a 'rodent catcher'.

In Ancient Egypt the cat was worshipped as the protector of their grain supplies. The Egyptian god of war, Sekmet, was often depicted as a lion, the big cat, said to be kin of the little cat Bastet or Pasht, depicted as a cat-headed woman. The Sun God, Ra, was worshipped in the form of a cat. There is a papyrus picturing Ra, a giant cat, with a knife beheading Apop the serpent of darkness. The Pharaohs in about 1000 BC made Bubastis their capital and the centre of the Bastet cult, and domestic cats became sacred to Bast. They were pictured on tombs, and carvings show them sitting under chairs, sometimes tied by ribbons to chair-legs. We see them eating fish, holding mice, and retrieving wildfowl from a marsh. Bronze figures of Egyptian cats are to be found in museums all over the world.

The Egyptians valued their cats highly; the penalty for killing a cat was death. There is a story of a Roman soldier who killed a cat and was himself almost torn to death by an Egyptian mob. The cat was one of the first possessions to be rescued in a disaster, and when the family cat died the family went into mourning, shaving off their eyebrows. Cats were buried with all the ceremony of a human funeral; they were embalmed with drugs and spices. A poor man's cat was rolled in plain linen but a rich man's cat would be bound in in strips of coloured linen, wound and pleated into elaborate patterns. The head was covered with a papier-mâché mask with linen discs for eyes, and ears formed from the midribs of palm leaves. The body was then placed in a mummy case of precious wood or precious metal, bejewelled, and placed in a tomb. Kittens were buried in small bronze coffins, and small bowls of milk and food, sometimes mice, were buried with them. There were several cat cemeteries, the most famous in Bubastis, but the cats buried at Beni Hassan came to an ignoble end when in 1888 a farmer dug into their burial ground. Most of the cemetery's contents were sold for fertiliser. Nineteen tons of mummified cat bones were shipped to England to be made into fertiliser. It

An Egyptian cat.

8

has been estimated that this consignment alone represented about 80,000 cats.

Although the Egyptians jealously guarded their cats and forbade their export, by the fifth century cats were popular in Persia, Burma, India and Siam. The cat was beloved and revered by the prophet Mohammed and is still regarded as sacred by Hindus and Muslims. Cats were kept in the temples to guard the shrines and to keep down the rats which might destroy precious manuscripts. In the National Library in Bangkok today are manuscripts saved from the ancient city of Ayudha, Siam's former capital. One of them, *Cat Book Poems*, illustrates and describes the cats seen in the years between 1350 and 1750 when Ayudah was destroyed.

In the Malayan Peninsula, the cat was used in rain-making rituals. In China, figures of cats were placed on the eaves of houses to repel demons. In Japan, cats were thought to contain the souls of ancestors. Near Tokyo there is a temple where priests sing chants for the souls of cats and cat images ornament the façade of the temple. Maneki-Neko raises its right paw in welcome. The Beckoning Cat is a popular charm in Japan. There is a legend telling how at one time the temple was very poor and the monks half-starved. The master-priest had a little cat who shared his food. One day the cat was sitting by the roadside and along came some cavaliers on splendid horses. The little cat raised one of its paws as if beckoning to them. They pulled up and followed the cat into the temple. Then came torrential rain so the priest gave them tea and expounded the Buddhist doctrine. Afterwards, one of the cavaliers, Lord Li, came regularly to receive religious instruction. Eventually he endowed the temple with a large estate, which became the property of his family, and in the beautifully laid-out gardens near the Li family cemetery is the little shrine of the beckoning cat. The Peruvians had a feline god, and the Irish had a god with a cat's head. The Norse goddess Freya had a chariot drawn by two cats.

In the Middle Ages, the cat as god was to become the cat as devil. Cats fell from favour and were persecuted, tortured and burnt. The Knights Templar were accused of worshipping the Devil in the form of a black tomcat. In 1484 Pope Innocent VIII gave powers to the Inquisition to seek out and burn cat-worshippers. Cats were dipped in oil and set on fire, they were flung from towers on feast days and beaten to death, crucified, scalded and skinned alive. On St John's Day, throughout Europe, cats were put into sacks and thrown into a bonfire. Cats were believed to be affiliated with Satan, and at the Coronation of Elizabeth I cats were stuffed into a wicker-work effigy of the Pope, paraded through the streets and then thrown into the bonfire. Cats were subjected to horrible cruelty in many ways. The terrible cat organs were invented and were in use for over a hundred years. Twenty cats were confined in narrow cases in which they could not move, and their tails were tied by cords to the keyboard of the organ. When the keys were pressed the cords were jerked and the cats' tails were pulled, making the cats cry out. It is said that this device was invented in 1549 for a festival in honour of Philip II, and a great bear, as the musician, pounded on the keys.

In Scotland, practised until the end of the eighteenth century, was the cat-ritual of Taigh-eirm. This atrocious ceremony lasted four days and four nights. The cats that were sacrificed had to be black, and they all had to be slowly tortured. Each cat was put on a spit and roasted before a slow fire. The moment its howling ceased in death, another cat took its place; there could be no break in the continuity. During the rite, infernal spirits appeared in feline form and their unearthly cries mingled with the shrieks of the cats on the spit. Finally an enormous cat would appear and the operator would demand his reward for his sacrifice. Very often the gift of second sight was asked for and granted and this was retained until his death.

There was a saying 'they are going to kill the cat', signifying the finishing of the harvest, and when the last corn was cut they killed a cat in the farmyard. At threshing time a live cat was placed in the last bundle of corn to be threshed and was struck dead with the flail, to be roasted and eaten on Sunday.

Cats were 'familiars' of witches and witch-

CATTY CURIOSITIES.

A Page from the Editor's Scrap Album.

CRYSTAL PALACE CAT SHOW, 1872.

ODE.

Addressed to a favourite Cat.

I.
POOR Puss! what tranquil days are thine!
　How happy, and how few!
While man—Creation's lord, is tried
　By evils ever new.

II.
Thy wants are small, thy wishes rare,
　Content—thy humble lot;
No *pride* distinguishes to thee
　The palace from the cot.

III.
And cannot man, proud man, restrain
　His murmurs, fears, and sighs?
Was reason giv'n to be a curse,
　Destroying all our joys?

IV.
His wants are few—his wishes great,
　Beyond their proper sphere;
Pride mocks Contentment—mars his peace,
　While comforts disappear.

V.
Let reasoning man instruction learn
　From emblems such as these;
Then shall his wishes too be few,
　His mind shall rest at ease.

BILL EXHIBITED IN LONDON THIRTY-FIVE
YEARS AGO.

CATS' SUPPER FIFTY YEARS AGO.

CATS' SUPPER TO-DAY.　Louis Wain.

hunts were carried on for over three hundred years. Women were put to death as witches as late as the latter part of the eighteenth century. In Germany 100,000 witches were killed in the sixteenth century and the seventeenth century, 75,000 died in France, and another 30,000 were burned, hanged or drowned in Great Britain. Heaven knows how many hundreds of thousands of cats died with them.

In a small Cotswolds village is a museum depicting witchcraft through the ages; one model shows the kitchen of a Lancashire witch, complete with black cat. The witch is said to have died in 1928. Black magic is still practised today, so it is possible that cats are still sacrificed too. It has been reported that the countryside in York County, Pennsylvania, was swept by a terror of witchcraft as recently as 1929. The inhabitants, to make peace with the devil, plunged a live black cat into boiling water and kept one of its bones as an amulet.

At the height of the witch-hunting, the cat was an outcast and looked upon as the devil incarnate. Black cats especially were associated with Satan. It is to be wondered at that the cat was not exterminated during these cruel times.

By the time of the Renaissance, cats were welcomed back into the home. Since the first domestication in Egypt, the cat had proved useful to man; it was a protector of the grain harvest, a hunter and killer, and a 'furry mousetrap'. Rats and mice are everywhere; they will eat almost anything and what they do not eat they foul. They carry disease; they spread plague (the Black Death was carried by the rats following the Crusaders returning home), and bubonic plague is still a smouldering menace throughout the world. As a god and as a devil the cat has been useful to man, and mankind has rewarded the cat with shelter and food. Because the cat is also warm and friendly, he has become a valued member of the family.

Cats are loved by the nobility and the poor alike. Queen Victoria had cats and even visited

Opposite: A page from *Our Cats*, May 4, 1901.

one of the early cat shows at the Crystal Palace. The young Louis XV permitted his kitten to play on the table during Royal Councils. Lord Chesterfield left pensions to his cats and their progeny. Very recently Princess Michael of Kent spoke on the radio about her nine cats.

Writers and artists had cats as pets. Richelieu had fourteen cats when he died. Heine, Walter de la Mare, Balzac, Victor Hugo, Thomas Hardy, Swinburne, Gray, T.S. Eliot – all these and many more wrote fondly of cats.

Many artists loved cats: Watteau, Picasso, Goya, Renoir, Manet. Gottfried Mind, sometimes called the Raphael of cats, was devoted to them and made many studies of them. Steinlein, famous for his posters, had a large colony of former stray cats in his Paris house. Henriette Ronner's pictures of cats reflect the life of the drawing-room, a life of ease and luxury, pampered pussies resting on velvet cushions. Steinlein's cats are working cats, the hunters, the chasers, the active cats, lithe and beautiful, his own strays. Many of the Dutch interiors include domestic cats, and portrait painters, such as Gainsborough, have painted the family cat in too. Nearly all families have a pet cat and most children are brought up on nursery rhymes and other children's stories about cats.

The popularity of the cat as a family pet is worldwide; they are beautiful, fastidiously clean, intelligent, loving and lovable. The company and affection of a cat gives solace to many lonely folk, and stroking the 'lap-cat' has a decidedly therapeutic benefit for many a sick person. Living with animals, especially a small animal like a cat, helps with the development of children's characters; they learn to care for and look after their pets, promoting a sense of responsibility and consideration. Cats are so adaptable that they can fit into most kinds of lives. The house-cat with complete freedom is happy to go out and come in, preferably to its own chosen routine and timetable; the flat-cat who never goes out will be content with a restricted life. Cats do adapt to a noisy household, put up with all kinds of musical instruments, watch television, befriend other pets and tolerate the hugging of children. Perhaps

'Maternal Bliss' by Henriette Ronner.

they prefer a quiet life, dozing by the fireside or more often, these days, asleep on a radiator, playing when they feel like it, eating when they are hungry and then sleeping again. They do not mind if the house is small, or large, one room only or a multitude of rooms, a garden or just a backyard – they will fit in.

Some families have pedigree cats – officially recognised breeds; but in most households the cat will be any of the many varieties and colours that have been around since the days of *Felis catus*: all the different tabbies, blacks or black and white, 'magpie-cats', grey-blue cats, ginger cats, torties, white cats, all-colour cats, fluffy or smooth cats.

This ever-increasing interest in cats, both pedigree and household pets, is measured to some extent by the interest in cat-breeding and cat shows. Thousands of kittens (it must be millions worldwide) are registered every year. More and more people are taking up the breeding of pedigree cats, cat clubs abound and there are no longer sufficient Saturdays in the year to accommodate the ever-increasing number of cat shows organised. This book sets out to describe the world of cat showing in all its aspects, and to convey the delight that cats of all kinds can give.

Above: 'Round the World' by Henriette Ronner.

Below: Illustration from *The Graphic*, July 22, 1871.

The picture opposite of an early Longhair poses a problem. In Harrison Weir's book *Our Cats and All About Them* (1889) is the following:

This Cat was the Property of Mrs Finch, of Maldon, Essex. In the Account of this Lusus Maturae, for such it may be deemed, the Mother has no other Likeness of her Production, than her Colour, which is a tawny Sandy, in some parts lightly streaked with black; she had this, and another Kitten like it, about two Years since. . . . This is a Male, above the usual Size, with a shaggy Appearance round its face, resembling that of the Lion's, in Miniature. The Hair protruding from the Ears, formerly grew, like what are termed Cork-screw Curls, and which are frequently seen, among the smart young Watermen, on the Thames; the Tail is perfectly distinct from that of the Cat Species, and resembles the Brush of a Fox. . . . The Proprietor has been offered, and refused, One Hundred Pounds for this Animal.

In *Our Cats* magazine of December 1957 (now defunct) was the following with the same picture featured:

A LANDSEER CAT

The engraving of the head and tail of a long-haired cat . . . cost a shilling on a London street barrow, perhaps because it was not realized the artist was Edwin Landseer.

Landseer drew it in 1912 when he was only ten years old and it was engraved by his brother Tom who was seven years his senior.

Landseer was an infant prodigy and excellent studies of animals by him made from the age of five onwards are preserved. Although he produced two mature works in which cats figure, 'The Cat's Paw' and 'The Larder Invaded', it was for his portrayal of *Felis leo* rather then *Felis catus* that he became famous.

A biographer records that late in life, when honours had been heaped upon him, Landseer was shown a drawing of a Persian cat, possibly this one, which he had made in 1812. He playfully annotated the drawing: Sketched at Maldon by the little boy Edwin when ten years old, and now Sir E. Landseer, an old boy 1866.

Breeders will be interested to note how greatly the shape of the 'Persian' cat's head has changed in 150 years.

The above was written by Sidney Denham, a breeder and writer, with his wife, Helen Denham, who was also a judge. The picture is the same in both instances with the connecting link being Maldon. I wonder where the original sketch is now.

2 The Origins of Showing 1871-1906

The first official Cat Show was held at the Crystal Palace, a very famous building built in Hyde Park, London, for the Great Exhibition of 1851, with thousands of panes of glass being used in its construction. It was the brainchild of Albert, the Prince Consort of Queen Victoria. After the Exhibition it was to have been demolished, but instead it was decided to move it out of the park and rebuild it elsewhere. The chosen place was near Sydenham, in the south-east, a suburb of London, where it proved a very popular venue for various exhibitions and shows. For many years it was to be the venue for cat shows, at first under the management of the Crystal Palace, and later organised by the National Cat Club.

The person responsible for the first Official Cat Show was Harrison Weir, a Fellow of the Horticultural Society, an artist and writer, and also a great cat lover. Writing in 1904 about the first cat show which was held on Thursday, 13 July, 1871, he said that when 'thinking of the great number of cats kept in London alone, I conceived the idea that it would be well to hold "cat shows", so that the different breeds, colours, markings, etc. might be more carefully attended to, and the domestic cat, sitting in front of the fire, would then possess a beauty and an attractiveness to its owner unobserved and unknown because uncultivated her-etofore.' He was not a man to let grass grow under his feet, and soon went to see Mr Wilkinson, the then manager of the Crystal Palace. He said 'it was a thing to be done.' Harrison Weir went home and in a few days was ready with all the details, and presented his scheme in full working order. He had worked out 'the schedule of prizes, the price of entry, the number of classes, and the points by which they would be judged, the number of prizes in

each class, their amount, the different varieties of colour, form, size and sex for which they were to be given. I also made a drawing of the head of a cat to be printed on black or yellow paper for a posting bill.' From then on, things really began to move. Mr F. Wilson, the company's naturalist and show manager, took charge and by working hard 'got a goodly number of cats together'. Included in the entry was Mr Weir's blue tabby, The Old Lady, then fourteen years old, which eventually won the best in the show of its colour. She won a little silver bell, which Mr Weir wore on his watch chain until he died.

The three judges were the Rev. J. Macdona, Mr Weir's brother John Jenner Weir, and Harrison Weir himself.

Harrison Weir, from *The Book of the Cat* by Frances Simpson, Cassell & Co. Ltd, 1903.

Manx, or Tailless Cat
British Wild Cat

Persian Cat
English Cat—the Biggest in the Show

Siamese Cats
French-African Cat

PRIZE CATS

Illustration from *The Graphic*, July 22, 1871, following the first Cat Show at the Crystal Palace.

On the day of the judging he confessed that he felt anxious when journeying up to judge at the show, and wondered what it would be like, how many cats would be there, and how the cats would behave in their cages. He wondered whether 'they would sulk or cry for liberty, refuse all food, or settle down and take the situation quietly and resignedly, or give way to terror? I could no way picture to myself the scene; it was all so new.'

On the train he met a friend who told him that he hated cats and drove them away from his premises when he saw them. Mr Weir told him that he had 'instituted the Cat Show as he wished everyone to see how beautiful a well-cared for cat is, and how docile, gentle, and – may I use the term? – cossety.' He persuaded the friend to come to the Cat Show with him.

When they entered the hall they found the cats quietly reclining on crimson cushions, and there was no noise or struggling to escape, while many of the cats were purring, and lapping the 'nice new milk provided for them'. The friend said he had no idea there were so many colours and sizes. A month or two later he called on his friend when he was at lunch, and found he now had two cats sitting on a chair beside him! He was pleased to observe that 'this was not a solitary instance of the good of the first Cat Show in leading up to the observance and kindly feeling for the domestic cat.'

The show was well publicised and the day before the show various national newspapers carried the following advertisement:

CRYSTAL PALACE – CAT SHOW
The first show of Domestic and other CATS will be opened in the CRYSTAL PALACE TOMORROW (Thursday) at ten o'clock. It will

17

consist of 25 classes, comprising nearly all the known species of Eastern and other foreign domestic cats, as well as the British Varieties, exhibited for their beauty of colour, form, weight and condition. The show will close at 7 p.m. Admission to the Palace and to the Show one shilling or by Guinea Season.

I should point out here that Eastern was the name given to the longhaired cats, as they came from Turkey or Persia, and the British were shorthaired. Some years later Harrison Weir was to complain that the Eastern cats had ousted the British (his favourites) out of favour.

The public turned up in such numbers that apparently at times it was impossible to see the cats at all. The number exhibited was 170, and the prizes distributed, 54 in all, amounted to £57 15s. On the morning of the show *The Daily Telegraph* urged its readers 'to hurry down to the Crystal Palace as soon as they read these lines', and hurry down they did so that the attendance of visitors was, as it turned out, inconveniently large.

The exhibition was held in the north nave of the Crystal Palace, and the cats were penned in cages belonging to the Peristeronic Club, which was part of the Pigeon Society. One reporter wrote that 'the dog has his day and makes a terrible noise; but the cat will do anything but miaow at the Crystal Palace. There never was such a noiseless show. Some of the cats were said to be somnolent as dormice, while others were quietly engaged in nursery affairs, being accompanied to the exhibition by very young kittens.' To this day, visitors to a show are always amazed at the quietness of the hall, especially if they have been to a dog show previously.

The cats were penned according to colour, with prizes being given for the best tortoiseshell, the black and white, for the longhaired or Persian cats, and for the heaviest weight. They were judged according to the points as worked out by Harrison Weir, that is for elegance of form, richness of colour and beauty, and evenness of markings. The standards that he set all those years ago are still very similar to those used at shows today. Many thought that the best and most beautiful of cats were the white Persians, several of which with 'their pale blue eyes, looked as if they had no business to be out of fairyland'. The prize for the fattest cat, which weighed over 20 pounds, went to Mr Nash's cat, whereas that for the biggest was won by a 'fine brown tabby' belonging to a Miss Amos. A richly-coloured sandy tom took another first prize. One of the exhibits was a 'French African' or Algerian cat, and there were several Manx entered. Another cat said to be direct from Persia was remarkable for his beautiful black, grey and white coat. He was said also to be very amiable.

A British Wild Cat was exhibited by the Duke of Sunderland, and *The Graphic* wrote: 'This cat is very scarce, indeed almost extinct in the British Islands. The colour is sandy-brown, and the form at the end of the nose and tail peculiar. He has lost the front right paw. He behaved like a mad devil, and ten men could not get him into a wire cage out of the box in which he was sent.' Another paper wrote that the poor creature 'was bristling with passion — who gathers himself up in a corner of his cage and glares at the public with his wrinkled yellow face, occasionally making a fierce dash against the bars of the cage, beating his head in ungovernable fury.' Two stuffed ones were also on show.

It is amusing to read of the different descriptions of the two Siamese at the show. *The Graphic* wrote that they were 'soft fawn-coloured creatures, with jet black legs, an unnatural nightmare kind of cat'. Another writer wrote that they were 'singular and elegant in their smooth skins, and ears tipped with black, and blue eyes with red pupils'. They were described, too, as being like black-faced pug dogs. They were thought to have been the first brought to Britain.

It appears to have been a two-day show, although it does not seem to have been advertised as such, but one report said that the judges did their judging on the first day, and the public were admitted on the second.

Another report said that 'one myth has been

cleared up by the exhibitors, namely that cats and spinsters are always associated.' Of the prizes awarded '32 were won by gentlemen, 15 went to married ladies, and only 4 to spinsters.'

The Illustrated London News gave full coverage to the show with many drawings of the exhibition, saying: 'It is two or three weeks since a pigeon race to Brussels was the special attraction at the Crystal Palace. This has been followed by an exhibition of domestic cats. At first the proposal to hold a cat show was received with much ridicule; but nothing succeeds like success. The number of entries and the multitude of visitors are sufficient guarantee that a cat show will in future constitute in the annual attractions of the Palace.' *The*

How *The Illustrated London News* of July 22, 1871, depicted the first Cat Show.

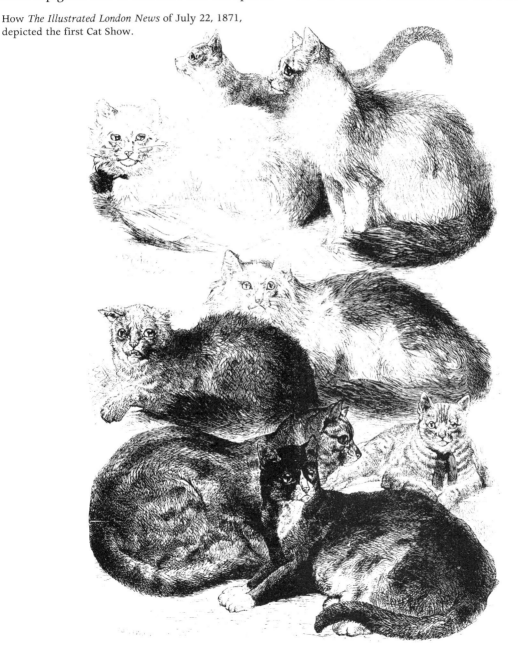

Illustrated Times wrote that 'the rage for shows has surely nearly reached its climax. The public have long been familiar with flower shows, cattle shows, dog shows, and shows of agricultural instruments and produce. There have been baby shows and at least one barmaid show. AND now we have got a cat show, and a very successful show it appears to have been. There was a wealth of cat that must have astonished those who are ignorant of the beauty and varieties of the animal.'

John Jennings wrote in *Domestic or Fancy Cats* (1893): 'My first associations with cats from a fancy point of view was at the Crystal Palace in 1871. Many will remember the sensation created by this first Cat Exhibition, which opened up a channel for the feline race never hitherto dreamt of. Many who then were seized with 'cat fever' will recollect how this first programme was subjected to criticism. "The very idea of a Cat Show." The usual wisdom after events have been successful was of course strongly in evidence.'

The show was such a success that the Directors of Crystal Palace arranged very quickly for another one to take place in December. Naturally Harrison Weir was very pleased with the results, but as most of the exhibitors were obviously monied people he made the comment that 'it was hoped that some means might be taken of promoting the exhibition of cats by the working classes.' This did eventually happen.

The first show was judged according to the points of excellence worked out by Mr Weir, but it is interesting to read the following from the *Christian Miscellany and Family Visitor* as early as 1846, as the cats described then were the ancestors of the cats at the first show:

> There are four distinct races of cats; namely, the tabby which includes the black cats, and which is nearly allied to wild kinds; the tortoiseshell cat, which came originally from Spain, and the males of which are buff with stripes of darker hue; the white and light coloured cats, which have reddish eyes, and a greyish tint in their fur, and are descended from the Chartreuse breed; and the Angora cats, which are quite distinct from all

others and are known by their long fur. The tailless cats of Cornwall and the Isle of Man belong to the Chartreuse breed and are the ugliest of their kind, as the Angora are the handsomest.

The 1871 show proved to be the foundation stone for all the Cat Fancies throughout the world. In Britain shows followed one another in rapid succession, sometimes on their own or in conjunction with Agricultural shows, and also with dog shows. There were no cat clubs and no official registering of cats and kittens, although many fanciers must have kept records of their own breeding.

After a cat show at the Alexandra Palace in 1887, a number of fanciers got together and decided it was time to start a club, and so the National Cat Club was formed, although it was eventually a governing body. It kept a register of cats, granted championships, and in 1893 issued the first stud book. Clubs ran shows under its rules and regulations. Harrison Weir was the first President, and the various vice-presidents' and the committee's names seemed to have come straight out of *Debrett*.

In 1890 a journal, *Fur and Feather*, was published, with pages on rabbits, birds, cavies and cats. Clubs were asked to send in reports of their meetings, and a show held in Kew Gardens in 1890 was mentioned, but it gave only the names of the people exhibiting and not those of the cats. The idea took off rather slowly at first, but soon cat fanciers did respond by sending in articles, advertising kittens and males at stud, and articles on cats, mostly longhaired. It was not to become the official organ of the GCCF until 1919.

Crufts' Dog Show is now world famous, but few people realise that in 1894 Crufts ran a cat show. It was known as Crufts' Great International Cat Show, and was held in St Stephens Hall, the Royal Aquarium, London on 7–8 March. It is difficult to know why it was called 'International' as the only exhibit that came from overseas was from Ireland.

It attracted good publicity, with the Great Northern and the Midland railways taking full page advertisements in the catalogue and pro-

This appeared in *The Illustrated Sporting and Dramatic News* of June 25, 1887.

viding a through van from Inverness, and they even had a representative at the show to give help to exhibitors. The return fare for fanciers from Wolverhampton was 7s.6d.

It was a two-day show open to the public until 10 p.m. There were four judges, Harrison Weir and his brother John, John Jennings, author of *Domestic and Fancy Cats* published in 1893, and a Miss Gresham, about whom nothing is known. The judges must have had plenty to do, as there were 567 exhibits, in 74 classes, with the brace class having 30 pairs entered, which meant 60 cats just in one class for one of the poor judges. The prizes were 30s. for a first, 20s. for second and 10s. for third. The specials really were special, as some cups costing up to 25 guineas were won outright, and a gold medal was given to the team winners. A team was for three exhibits. One exhibit went home with two cups, £3 in cash, a silver cigarette case, a silver whistle and a medal.

There was another weekly paper at the beginning of the century – *Our Cats*, which sold for 1d. It carried advertisements at 12 words for 4d and a cattery register for 2 lines at 3d. It gave details of cat meetings, show reports and was

Louis Wain's impressions of the 1892 Crystal Palace Cat Show, from *The Illustrated Sporting and Dramatic News*, October 22.

really quite comprehensive. As in those days there was no ban on cats being called after famous people, there were such announcements as 'General Gordon and his children have done well in the show pen', or 'the Duke of Kent is at stud for £1.1.0d.', but that 'the Duke of Gloucester was disqualified at a show for being under age'.

One could read that Kaiser Wilhelm's keen hatred of cats was 'the cause of their being taxed in Germany and if pussy does not wear a medal showing she is fully licensed an unsentimental policeman hurries her off to the lethal chamber.' The licence cost was 1s. for one cat and 3s. for two.

The appalling death rate of cats and kittens after the show makes horrendous reading. No one seemed to realise that death was due to a killer illness, now known as feline infectious enteritis, and everything was blamed: shows too hot or too cold, wrong feeding at the show, bad handling, poison, travelling upsets, or the pens. Crystal Palace Company went as far as to issue a statement that their pens were always cleaned, as was the tabling, and could in no way be blamed for all the deaths. Post-mortems were sometimes carried out and reported on as distemper, gastro-enteritis, and show fever. This went on for years as there were no inoculations available then for cats and kittens. In fact it was not until after World War 2 that there were any.

Whole catteries were wiped out and many breeders and cat owners refused to exhibit at all. The sad thing was that when people's kittens or cats died they would immediately get others, only to have them die within a very short time. No one realised that the infection was still in the house. Judges did not wear overalls and very little thought seemed to have been given to hand washing. There was no disinfectant as we now know it. The year 1912 was disastrous to a number of cat breeders, and the editor of *Our Cats* wrote: 'What is to be done? Must cat shows cease? Must kittens or young cats never be exhibited? Or is it possible . . . that science may discover the cause of the evil, and consequent on the discovery the remedy may be given to the fancy.'

It was not surprising that infection did run rife, as kittens back from a show mixed with the others in the household, with the result that they died as well. The Newbury Cat Show manager had the bright idea of making exhibitors sign a declaration that to their knowledge their exhibits had not been in contact with any infectious disease for 14 days, but this seemed to have little effect. Even when fanciers gave up showing, they still accepted queens to their studs, often from breeders that had just lost kittens. In those early days the only disinfectant that seems to have been mentioned is eucalyptus. In addition, shows were held on different days of the week, and cats and kittens could almost go from one show to another as there were many shows throughout the country.

Fleas were a great problem and various powders were tried, many so strong that they tended to kill the kittens as well as the fleas. One well advertised and which may well have had some effect was Mothaline, an 'insect exterminator of fleas and lice'. It was said to be the best, with fanciers quoted as saying that 'no other insect powder kills like it on earth'. In among the advertisements for kittens there appears one for hedgehogs at 1s each or 1s 6d a pair which were said to be invaluable for killing beetles, obviously another problem.

In spite of everything cat shows did go on and increased rapidly, until it seemed that every county in Britain had at least one cat show.

After the first show society took up cats with great enthusiasm, especially as it was known that both Queen Victoria and the Prince of Wales (later Edward VII) were cat lovers and attended one or two of the earlier shows, with the Prince presenting photographs of himself to the owner of the Best Cat. The Queen owned cats as well as dogs, and had two blue Persians. She gave one of her kittens, Duschar, to HRH Princess Victoria of Schleswig-Holstein, her granddaughter, and this cat later won a number of prizes.

A number of shows were held at the Aquarium in Brighton, Sussex, which proved to be a very popular venue, but 1900 was the last one when it was taken over by the local authorities. Going back to 1873 there was a show in Newbury and another in Birmingham, but one writer obviously did not think much of them, as he said rather disparagingly that to win a VHC (very highly commended) at the Crystal Palace was as good as a first prize elsewhere.

By 1902 Harrison Weir had retired from his connections with the Cat Fancy, and fanciers banded together to present him with a testimonial, but the response could not have been what was expected. Writing in *Our Cats* in that year he regretted he had not been unable to acknowledge his testimonial before as he had been too unwell. He wished to thank all his 'warm-hearted and truly unforgetful friends that had contributed.' He could not have been very impressed, as he went on to say 'Though they are indeed somewhat small in number . . . though few out of the boundless many, thanks again . . . and may their lives and days be bright and long in the land.' I think by this time he had become disillusioned with some fanciers who thought more of winning cups than they did of their cats. He was also disappointed that the shorthaired English cats (now referred to as British) had been neglected for the Foreign longhairs (the Angoras and Persians). He considered the English cats far more intelligent than the longhairs, and blamed the judges who went for compactness rather than line, which resulted in the shorthairs being bred too short in the leg. He went on to say he much preferred the cats as they had been 50 years ago. This was years before he thought of the first cat show, so although I am sure he would not have agreed he was in one way responsible for this, as the cat shows promoted great interest in cat breeding.

The early 1900s saw a spate of clubs being formed, as the interest in pedigree cats and showing was growing all the time. Apart from the National Cat Club in 1887, and the Scottish Cat Club in 1894 which ran many shows in Glasgow, the fanciers could now join a number of clubs, such as the Siamese Cat Club, the Northern Counties Cat Club, the Midland Counties Cat Club, and various specialist clubs such as the Blue Persian, the Silver and Smoke, the Black and White, and several others, nearly all of which were soon running shows of their own under the rules and regulations laid down by the National Cat Club. Things went very well for a while, with some of the original clubs amalgamating with one another. In 1898 Lady Marcus Beresford had formed the Cat Club, which also decided to register cats and issue a stud book, and there was rivalry among the fanciers. There was much correspondence on the subject in the pages of *Our Cats*, with people and even clubs taking sides. In 1901 the National decided to disqualify or prohibit from winning prizes at their shows all cats registered after July 1 at any club but the National. This edict prompted even more letters to *Our Cats*. The Cat Club ran shows at Richmond and Westminster, giving most of the proceeds to charity, including the families of soldiers killed in the South African War, and £100 to the Great Ormond Street Children's Hospital. Attempts were made for the two clubs to amalgamate, but no satisfactory solution was found. In 1904 the Cat Club show lost £113 and the club was wound up shortly afterwards.

In 1909 another registered body came into existence, known as the Incorporated Cat Fanciers Association of Great Britain, which took over the liabilities of an Association (CFA) which had come into being the year before, but did not seem to be very successful. Notabilities in the Cat Fancy, such as Frances Simpson, author of *The Book of the Cat*, breeder and show manager, and Mr R.H.W. Biggs were amongst them. There was general unrest throughout the Cat Fancy, and the National Cat Club decided to take the first steps to try to solve the situation. Three delegates from the new Association were invited to meet three from the National Cat Club to sort out the troubles. Nothing seems to have come out of this meeting, and clubs continued to press for some say in the running of the Cat Fancy and the shows.

On March 11 1910 representatives from the various clubs were invited to a meeting in London, and it was decided to form a Council, which was to be known as the Governing Council of the Cat Fancy. The National Cat Club agreed to hand over all rights of registering, issuing of stud books, and transfers, being given the right to have four delegates on the council in perpetuity. Attempts have been made over the years to question this right, but it was recognised that the National did have certain rights, and it was said that any attempt to reduce the representation of the premier club would be resisted by the Chairman of the Council. The Midland Counties Cat Club, the Southern Counties, the Northern Counties (which ceased to function) and the Blue Persian (the only specialist cat club then to be granted two delegates) and the others mentioned were as founder members granted the right to have two delegates in perpetuity. However it was agreed that other clubs could have further delegates as their membership increased, rather than just one as agreed formerly.

The Governing Council of the Cat Fancy revised its constitution in 1932 when it was agreed that all the original clubs which had been allowed more than one delegate already should keep them even if the number of members fell below the stipulated minimum. This ruling still stands. Recently in the Cat Fancy another Association has come into being which is running shows and registering cats, and also choosing its own judges. It is known as the Cat Association, but the GCCF does not accept officials of that Association as delegates to the Council, nor may GCCF judges judge at the Association's shows.

To go back to the early 1900s, the so-called show fever seemed to be more virulent than ever, with hundreds of cats and kittens dying. 1900 was a very bad year, and when a Mr Townsend, who had been involved with the Crystal Palace shows, took over the running of the National Show in 1901, he arranged for two veterinary surgeons to examine all the exhibits, and had the show disinfected with Emeryl, which had been recommended. These precautions seemed to be of little use, and the next year too was just as bad, but fanciers still continued to show young kittens.

Cats and kittens could be sent unaccompanied to the shows, with the collection being arranged for by the show manager, who had to pen and feed them, and arrange for their return. There were occasions when the cats arrived late at the station and missed the show altogether. One manager, writing about the return of the cats, said that 'the show would be cleared at the time stated and any delay will lie at the door of the railway companies, who in spite of all precautions occasionally do fearful and wonderful things with live stock.'

After a show at Sandy, the show manager, Mr Western, wrote a letter complaining of the unsatisfactory way some of the cats sent to the show were packed. Apparently it was quite a common thing for cats to arrive in margarine boxes etc with the lids nailed down. Things were improving, he thought, but cats were still arriving with the baskets tied up with endless bits of string. He said that show hampers should always be fastened with straps or rods, as they were safer, and saved the stewards who had to unpack and repack the cats endless trouble.

A very successful show was held at Cheltenham in November 1906, but there was a great deal of grumbling because the cats were not separated from the poultry and rabbits.

With a view to reducing the mortality in kittens the National Cat Club passed a rule that no kittens under six months should be shown, but at the same time raised the kitten age to twelve months. The Southern Counties Cat Club had divided views on this subject and held a plebiscite that resulted in the majority voting in favour of running their own show and not under National Cat Club rules, which meant no championships could be awarded. The ruling seemed to be generally frowned on and was soon rescinded.

Everything seemed to go wrong before the 1907 Crystal Palace show when the show manager fell ill, and Dr Roper, the Chairman, wished to postpone the show, 'but it could not be', and he carried on as best he could. In return for which he was covered with abuse for doing his best to meet an extraordinary sequence of difficulties. A few days before the show he found they required 500 pens for the cats and kittens, and only had 350. Straw (used as bedding) and sawdust (used for the cats' toilet) had not been ordered. There was no heat because the Palace was out of coal, and finally the electric light failed as the cats were arriving. One can only hope that all went well afterwards.

Browsing through the old magazines, I was intrigued to read about the early cats' meat men, and to realise how much their services were appreciated and indeed needed by the Cat Fancy, as a whole. I was more than interested as I remember when I was a child in 1914 my mother giving me 2d to go out to buy meat for my Black Persian, Bobby, from the cats' meat man, who came around every week pushing a little wooden barrow, calling 'CATS' MEAT' at the top of his voice. I would rush out, with my cat following, as he always recognised the voice, and knew what it meant.

Chas Ross in his *Book of the Cats*, 1867, said that there were thought to be at least 200,000 cats in London, but there could be well over 300,000, as some houses took in lodgers who had cats, which could not be counted. One cats' meat man said he served as many as 200 cats, but only 70 dogs, with some cats having a ha'pence worth every day. Another said he had been in the business for over 25 years and reckoned that London alone bought about 200,000lb a week at 2½d per lb which worked out at £100,000 a year. There were considered to be about 1000 cats' meat carriers, so it really was big business, and was also doing much to help with the feeding of cats. This was before the time of cat shows and pedigree breeding.

As the number of pedigree cats grew, so did the trade, with the customers being most grateful for the service. In 1900, it was decided that appreciation should be shown in a practical way, and *Our Cats* started a fund to collect money to do something for 'these hard-working men, who from their stock would often throw scraps to any starving cats they happened to see.' The response from the magazine's readers was excellent and it was decided to hold a dinner with entertainment for about 150 men, and that Louis Wain would take the chair. The applicants had to be certified as genuine cats' meat men by their customers. The demand proved to be so great that the numbers were increased to 250 for the dinner, with 400 having to be refused.

The dinner was held in the Baronial Hall of a London restaurant. Louis Wain welcomed everyone and read a letter from the Princess of Wales (later Queen Alexandra) regretting that she could not be present but wished the occasion every success. It was reported that the men were in the best of spirits at the dinner and 'no one could have guessed that they were a body of cats' meat men . . . a class worthy of encouragement.' A surprise visitor, the Duchess of Bedford, made a speech and before departing gave instructions that each man was to be presented with a tin of tobacco valued as 2s.9d.

Afterwards the men were entertained by a number of well-known performers; one, a Mde Janotha, not only played the piano but also brought with her her famous black cat, White Heather, which had a great fuss made of it by the guests. Other performers included opera singers, and even Frances Simpson, the well-known cat judge, gave a solo song.

In January 1901 Queen Victoria died. She had reigned for 64 years and the whole nation went into mourning, even *Our Cats* was printed with a deep black band around the cover and inside was an eulogy, part of which was:

> It comes as a painful and solemn task to us to have to put on record the death of our beloved Queen. No one in the world has ever done so much for poor animals – no one in the world, and they will all miss her – miss her more, perhaps than even her sorrowing subjects.

In 1901 *Our Cats* started to print a *Who's Who of the Cat World*, giving the names of noted

Louis Wain, from *The Book of the Cat.*

exhibitors, breeders or persons of distinction. It started with the Countess of Aberdeen, followed by Sir Claude and Lady Alexander, and many others. It gave a list of cats they had bred, their position in the Cat Fancy, and also asked for a comment on their views of the cat world, some of which are well worth repeating. A Mrs H. Barnett said that she thought 'it desirable that gentleman judges should be appointed wherever possible, and great care should be exercised to see that judges are not acquainted with those exhibits they are judging,' Mrs G. Boutcher said: 'My idea is that there are a great deal too many disagreeablenesses among the different clubs and societies, and I should like to read of a little more harmony amongst fanciers.'

Mrs E. Cope wrote: 'I sincerely trust that before another season the sanitary show pen may become an accomplished fact and that the appalling death-roll which seems to inevitably follow our large shows may vanish beneath the stern hand of the reformer.' Dr Roper, Chairman of the National Cat Club committee, who exported prize-winning Blacks to the United States, was obviously very proud of his achievements, as he commented: 'The secret of my success as a cat fancier has been sparing no expense in stock and proper mating, together with well-built houses, and keeping them properly cleaned, and the cats groomed daily and fed on a mixed diet.'

Mr C. Witt, a breeder, judge and reporter said that 'the cat fancy is quite in its infancy; that it has come to stay, and once we get over the petty jealousies that exist, and judges and fanciers credited with better intentions generally than at present, we shall go on and prosper and better prices will be obtained for A1 specimens because of the greater healthier rivalry and competition.'

The Scottish Cat Fancy was doing well, and the 1875 show held in Edinburgh attracted an entry of 560 cats. Great publicity was given to a cat which had been rescued by a fireman from the ninth storey of a burning house and to a cat which was rescued by a cabman after it had been locked up in an empty house by a family which had moved away. One lady was so

impressed by his kindness that she presented the cabman with a new shelter for his rank. Nothing seems to have been given to the fireman who really was a hero. The Scottish Cat Club was founded in 1894 and ran a number of shows in Glasgow, but by 1901 shows were being held all over Scotland. There were at least twenty that year, some two-day shows, others one only, and a few in conjunction with dog shows. There were a number of breeders who did not exhibit at all, possibly because of the fear of infection, but produced many outstanding kittens, which when sold took prizes at the English shows, including Crystal Palace. The biggest show in 1901 was held in Waverley Market in Edinburgh, and Lady Alexander who lived in Sussex, but also had a house in Scotland, showed a number of cats, and won many prizes, which did seem a little unfair. Colin Campbell, a judge and breeder, said at that time that he believed 'that taking it as one, on the whole, the Scottish fancy is as earnest, as honest, and as hopeful a body of people as one could desire.'

Queen Victoria may have died, but with HRH Princess Victoria of Schleswig-Holstein being patron of the National, and a breeder of Chinchillas and Blue Persians, and her mother HRH Princess Christian being a cat lover also, and many nobility serving on club committees, cat shows seemed to have been almost social gatherings. Many titled ladies kept large catteries, with their exhibits being taken to the shows in open wagonettes or 'growlers' by members of the household staff. The owners would arrive later in the day in their carriages and pair; the ladies in beautiful gowns and the gentlemen in morning dress, complete with top hat and gloves. Sometimes the maids and footmen would bring picnic hampers and serve lunch. One fancier had an Indian attendant to look after her cats at the show, which was thought to be very exotic. Domestic help was plentiful, and many had staff just to look after, feed and groom the cats and kittens. Lady Marcus Beresford's name appeared frequently among the prizewinners, which was not surprising as she had about 160 cats at one time. She travelled all over the

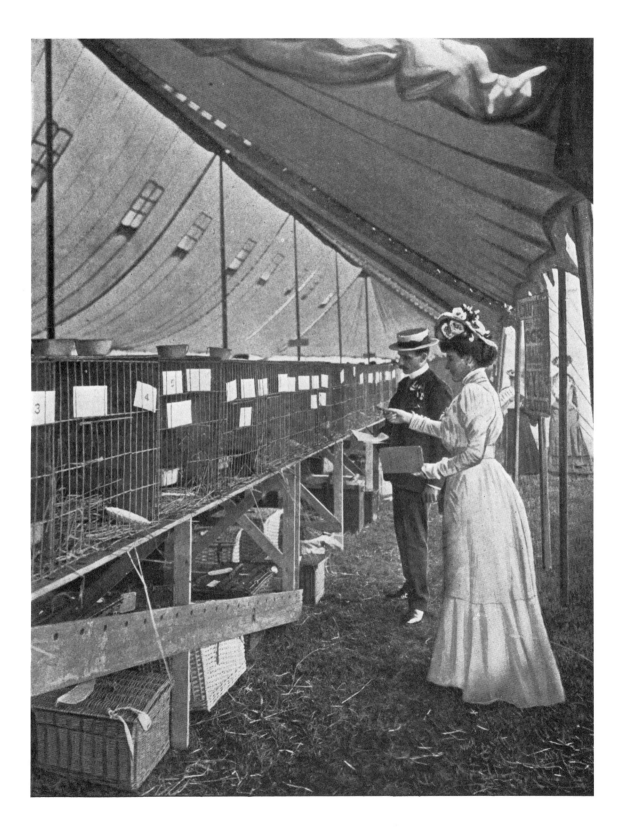

Early photographs of prizewinners at the 1903 Crystal Palace Show in *The Illustrated Sporting and Dramatic News* of November 7.

country, with her retinue, sometimes having more than 30 entries in one show.

At some shows there were ring classes similar to those at dog shows, with the owners walking around with their cats wearing brightly coloured ribbons. Often the cats were reluctant to walk and had to be dragged around, and at one show one famous stud cat flew at another, severely damaging his ear. There was panic all around, and one brave gentleman was badly scratched trying to separate the two cats. The class was very soon dropped from the shows.

Mr Townsend, who had been involved with the Crystal Palace Show before the National Cat Club took over, was once again show manager for the Club's 12th Show in 1901. In an endeavour to do something about the deaths following shows, he had the show disinfected with 'Emeryl'. It seemed of little help, as the loss was as bad as ever and even worse in 1902.

At the 1901 Show Sir Claude Alexander, a

Opposite: The 1902 Richmond Cat Show: judges at work (from *The Book of the Cat*).

well-known breeder of shorthairs, offered a £2 special for the best shorthaired male, female or neuter exhibited by a bona-fide working man. That year there were 120 classes, and the five judges included Louis Wain who judged the Tortoiseshells and the Tortie and Whites. Special classes were put on for working men's and woman's cats.

In 1902 there was a special Coronation Show to celebrate the crowning of King Edward VII. Harrods offered a special for the best white longhaired female with blue eyes at the show. There were over 200 exhibitors including the Princess Victoria, the Countess of Aberdeen, Lady Decies. The show was held in conjunction with the Ladies Kennel Association, and the proceeds were donated to charity. It was held in the Victoria Hall, London.

That year the King and Queen went on a Royal Tour and included a visit to the Isle of Man. Driving through one village, a Manx cat sitting on a wall was an interested spectator, and he attracted the attention of Queen Alexandra. Both their Majesties were very amused,

Prizewinners at the 1904 Show, from *The Illustrated London News* of November 5.

'Puck III' – the property of the Princess Victoria of Schleswig-Holstein (from *The Book of the Cat*).

so much so that before leaving the Island, they had asked for two of the breed to be sent to Balmoral and two more to Buckingham Palace.

The 1903 Crystal Palace Show attracted an entry of 450 cats, and instead of the show being held in a tent the cats were penned in a curtained-off part of the centre transept of the Palace. The entries included a Madagascar cat, looking like a monkey, a cat from Argentina that was spotted like a leopard, nineteen chinchilla cats and eleven kittens, very good blues, creams, blacks and Siamese.

By this time shows were being held all over Britain, ranging from small local shows with only forty cats being entered to the really big shows like the Palace. Many judges must have been needed, but it is rather difficult to find out how the early judges were appointed. The Blue Persian Society asked their members to put forward the names of suitable persons as judges, which were to be voted on by a postal ballot. At

A montage of the winning cats at the 1905 Crystal Palace Show, which appeared in *The Illustrated London News* on November 4.

the meeting eight names were given, but members could add further names if they wished. By 1903 the Society had 200 members, and supported shows all over the country, but did not run their own Championship Show until 1931, the second specialist club to do so, the Siamese having run their own show a few years earlier.

Show reports were beginning to appear in *Cats* magazine, but were very brief, i.e. 'Manx class (2 entered). 1. McEwens' – a typical Manx, good colour, head and eyes. 2. Simpson's rare red tabby good in markings.'

Clubs were being formed all over the country. In Scotland, in addition to the Scottish Cat Club, the Caledonian Cat Club came into being with the motto 'Equal rights for all members, no official loaves or fishes!' It held its first show in 1907, in Glasgow, but the rain fell in torrents 'which quite spoilt the gate.'

In one year there were 44 shows held throughout the country in the period August to November, 10 being on the same day.

Many of the clubs guaranteed classes at other clubs' shows, and at one show in Bath seven clubs were called on to pay up for the losses incurred on their classes, that is the entry money paid did not cover the prize money. The clubs complained that they had had to pay £8.7d. between them. There are still guaranteed club classes at some shows today, but they are rarely called on to pay anything.

As the interest in cats increased, a scientific experimenter decided to try to register on a phonograph 'the accents of cats', to find out about their language. He said that 'he was making progress and will have a syllabary and vocabulary which will let everybody into the secret of the language.' Unfortunately I cannot trace the results of his experiments anywhere.

Princess Victoria of Schleswig-Holstein continued to be interested in breeding and showing pedigree cats, and her father HRH Prince Christian gave her a birthday present of 'a lovely cat house for Puck (one of her male cats), with two rooms, a bedroom, and a living room. Puck has all his prize cards in the living room, and a photo of himself and all his children.'

The 1904 Crystal Palace show was said to be wonderful, with Ch. Zaida, a Silver Tabby, looking exquisite (£1,100 was refused for her), while 'Ch. Don Pedro of Thorpe seemed to enjoy ring judging, and behaved very well.' The band stopped playing while that class was being judged. Lady Decies' shorthaired blue kittens were thought 'perfect gems for beauty of head, colour, texture of coat and eyes.' The hall was said to be most attractive with the pens being prettily draped. Championships were given for the first time to the Orange and Cream cats. There was one complaint – a Mrs Shapcote complained that 'someone had taken her cat basket, and only left the label'. It was a white basket lined with pink flannelette, and she hoped that it would be returned.

The Scottish Cat Club show in Edinburgh that year did not seem to have gone too well, as only 50 pens were provided at first and more had to be found. The judges, Mrs McKenzie Stewart and Mr T. Mason, complained that the light was bad, and it was very unfair that they had too much to do, having to judge 415 entries between them.

In 1906 Silver Lambkin, the first Chinchilla stud, and winner of many prizes, died and was much mourned by the breeders. He was presented to the National History Museum at South Kensington, London, after being stuffed by a taxidermist, and was on exhibition there for many years. I saw him there in the early 1960s, and was in for a big disappointment. He was very dark, very short of coat, and did not look anything like the beautiful chinchillas seen at the shows today. When I went there again a few years ago, he was no longer on display.

As the shows increased in number, fanciers began to take more interest in breeding for specific colours, with longhairs becoming more and more popular. Clubs were anxious to have more say in the running of shows, but the formation of the Governing Council of the Cat Fancy in 1910 did seem to bring some uniformity to the Cat Fancy for a while at least. The world these early cat fanciers knew, however, was soon to change radically with the coming of the 1914–18 War, and things were never the same again.

3 The Development of Cat Shows in Great Britain

The establishment of the Governing Council of the Cat Fancy made for many changes in the cat world as more and more cat clubs were formed and became affiliated. This meant the licensing of more shows with many fanciers becoming interested in showing. *Our Cats* journal was now a monthly magazine and included the Gazette of the Governing Council of the Cat Fancy. It gave details of shows to be held under the GCCF rules, advertised the Stud Book which was available for 2s.6d. and printed a list of all the registrations for the past month.

By 1912 the GCCF were endeavouring to make a rule that there should be three weeks between the various shows. No reason is given, but it may have been with the hope of stopping some of the infection that was causing so many deaths, as 1912 was a very bad year. Unfortunately many clubs were against this ruling and fought it. They said that if it was passed they would hold their shows without the GCCF licence and this would mean no championships being given. The clubs must have won the day as there was no further mention of the rule. 1912 saw an epidemic of foot and mouth in Britain, with many agricultural shows being cancelled and also those with cat sections, such as Carlisle and Cumberland. The show at Sandy, which had become one of the first class shows, went ahead as usual, with Miss Simpson, Mrs Norris and Mr Mason being the judges. There were several shows held in Scotland, and one at Lanark was well run, even though the judging had to start late, as some of the trains bringing cats were one to two hours overdue.

That year Blue Russian and British kittens were offered for sale at 15s.6d. each, while the rare Abyssinians were five guineas a pair for show specimens. The Blue Persian Cat Society's accounts showed a 'very healthy balance' of

Pictures of the Southern Counties' Cat Club Show, from *The Illustrated Sporting and Dramatic News*, January 25, 1913.

Mrs. Power-Potts,
With her brown tabby Persian, "Spitfire."

Miss Jay's giant tabby, Ashley Abbott,
The weight of which is twenty-five pounds.

Mrs. G. New with her blue neuter, Séte of Egypt,
1st and Slingsby Challenge Cup.

£77.10s.8d.; the Neuter Cat Society had £10.8s.10d., and was said to be in a healthy condition too; the Governing Council was paying out £50 for a Secretary and clerical assistance, £10 for office accommodation, and had a balance of £24.18s. for the year.

The 1913 Southern Counties Cat Club Show had 100 classes, and 250 cups and specials, while the Scottish show in Glasgow was increasing in size all the time. In spite of the war clouds the 66th Sandy show held on August 31 1914 was a great success, with 102 exhibits. Mr Yeates, who was later Chairman of the GCCF, wrote that 'the best war show was The Grand Patriotic Championship show held at the Wellington Hall, St Johns Wood on the 5th November, with the proceeds going to War Funds.'

There were five shows held the next year, including the Loyalty Championship show at the Hounslow Baths on October 13, with the profits going to the Blue Cross Fund. This show was held under the patronage of HH The Ranee of Sarawak, and the prizes were war loan vouchers.

In 1916 the National Cat Club held two shows, one in aid of the Red Cross Fund, with an entry of 280 exhibits, including 37 Blue long-hair cats, and the second at the Lambeth Baths in aid of the Star and Garter Home. This was to be the last show held until the War was over, with the Sandy show being the first in 1919.

The Cat Fancy picked up slowly, but the 1920s saw cat shows being held nearly every week somewhere in the country. Very little was reported about some of the shows, but at the Bedford Show held in the Belle Vue Barracks for two days there was a strict ruling that officiating judges were not allowed to exhibit in any section of the show. The ruling today is the same, except that they may exhibit in the pet cat section. 'Izal' was used to disinfect the show, but nothing is said as to whether it helped to cut down infection.

Mr Yeates wrote that the Southern Counties Cat Club show, the last of the big winter shows, had a very large entry. The committee worked nobly but had set themselves a very hard task. He thought that 150 classes were far too much for a one-day show. I wondered what he would

Miss Simpson's Brown Tabby 'Persimmon', from *The Book of the Cat*.

have thought of the National with 700 classes being judged on the one day, but we do have over 100 judges. The judges found it quite impossible to finish judging before the time of admission for the public. When the public was admitted the judges complained that they could not complete their task with the gangways crowded with exhibitors and visitors, and the hall was cleared again. Judging finished at a very late hour, and few of the specials could be put on the pens.

The majority of the shows today do not admit the public until 12 noon; however, the larger shows to help cover the heavy costs allow the public in all day, but the judges cope very well. I shudder to think what would happen at the National if all the public had to be turned out to allow the judges to finish. There would probably be a riot!

It appears that by 1926 the Cat Fancy had really recovered from the effects of the War, as the National Show was the biggest since 1913 with 332 exhibits, and all the catalogues were sold out very early on the second day.

It is amazing what can go wrong at a show, and as a show manager myself I am always worried if something does not go wrong beforehand in case it does on the day. Mrs Fosbery, one of the judges of the 1927 Thame show, reported that there was a large entry of good quality cats, but she was struck by the large number of empty pens and could not understand it. She waited twenty minutes before starting judging in case there were any late arrivals due to bad weather. When she finished she checked the catalogue and found that each cat entered in more than one class not only had a number for each class, but also several pens. I should imagine the show manager was a novice.

The National Crystal Palace show in 1927, organised by Mr Yeates, was said to be the largest and the finest since the War, with an entry of over 1,000, and a splendid attendance.

In 1928 the Siamese Cat Club's Fifth Show was held in Kensington. A bouquet was presented to Lady Cook, wife of Sir Edward Cook, the Financial Adviser to the King of Siam, who presented rosettes to the winners. In conversation some interesting facts emerged about the cats in their native country. 'It seems that the males are much darker than the cats in Britain, and the heads, though narrow and pointed, are shorter in the nose. Kinked tails are not unknown but are considered a defect, and cats with kinked tails are never seen in the Royal Palace. The Siamese minister in London was unable to attend having been summoned to Paris.'

In 1930 the Lancs and North Western Counties Cat Club Show in July was for members only, and the exhibitors acted as stewards or at least were allowed to present their own cats or kittens to the judge. This worked well at a small show, but would not be possible at the large ones.

More thoughts were being given to hygiene at the shows, and at the Kensington Show the judging tables were covered with new American cloth and each judge was provided with a towel soaked in disinfectant and a clean towel as well.

In pre-war days the small local shows with about six to twelve classes were considered to be the nursery of the Scottish Cat Fancy, and were greatly enjoyed and just as keenly contested as at the larger shows. For twenty years the Fancy there seemed to be dead (probably it was never revived after the 1914–18 War), but at the Glengarnock Fur and Feather Show in 1934 there were two classes put on for cats and kittens, and it was hoped that this would pave the way for a Scottish rebirth. It must have done, for Glasgow too held a show the following year and had a 'wonderful' entry of 150 considering the gap there had been, and which augured well for the Scottish Cat Club.

There must have been great excitement in Thame in 1935 at a fur and feather show, which included cats, when there was the spectacle of the huge tents being blown to ribbons by the gale, while others subsided gracefully amid a tangle of cordage. Live stock was hastily evacuated from tents before the inevitable catastrophe occurred, but the cat section managed to carry on in spite of what at first sight appeared to be insurmountable obstacles. It was soon realised that the cat tent would soon be going, and everyone rushed to pluck the cats to safety. A suggestion was made that the cats should be transferred to the poultry and pigeon tent which was still standing next to the cat tent, but a 30-foot rip appeared in the roof of that shortly after the cat tent had subsided.

Some genius suggested that the cats be put into the three motor coaches which were standing just outside the entrance barrier, and a move was made in that direction. However, the steward at the gate refused to let any exhibit pass out of the show ground, even though the coaches were only 20 yards away. After some delay permission was obtained, and a helpful driver moved the coaches into a suitable position. 'Each judge took possession of one, and work was started once again. Queues formed by the door of each coach, and the cats were taken out of their baskets as their numbers were called by the judges.'

For many years the National Cat Club had held two shows a year, one in June in the Botanical Gardens, Regents Park, London, and the other in October at the Crystal Palace. There was drama the night before the show in 1936 when the Palace was burned down, a blaze which could be seen for miles. Mrs Sharman, the show manager, calmly sent telegrams to all the exhibitors and simply transferred the show to another hall. She had searched London and managed to get the Paddington Baths. Spratts, who penned the early shows, rushed to get the pens there and the hall was ready, but the show had to be reduced from two days to one. The National has only had one-day shows since then. The Paddington Baths were used for the next two years.

Mr Yeates, Chairman of the GCCF, wrote an article in *Our Cats* saying that all fanciers should join a club and attend the Annual General Meeting, and so have a say in the running of the Fancy. There were only two specialist clubs running their shows, but there were eighteen affiliated clubs, so there was plenty of choice.

Mr Cyril Yeates organised the National Cat Club Show from 1923 to 1936, the two-day shows at the Crystal Palace, until it was burned

down, and then for two years at the Paddington Baths. His influence on the Cat Fancy was great. He compiled a Supplement for the first GCCF Stud Book, 1912–17, and the second one 1917–23. In 1921 he became a Blue Persian judge, and in 1926 Chairman of the Governing Council. He was a very kindly man, and knew a great deal about breeding, giving me good advice when I first came into the Cat Fancy. On his retirement, he became President of the Council. According to Kathleen Yorke, later Chairman of the GCCF, 'He guided the Council through the two world wars and was of invaluable assistance in helping it to weather the difficulties of those times.'

In 1939, in spite of the war clouds hanging over Europe, shows went on as usual in Exeter, Bradford, Nottingham, Kensington, and Bingley. The ever-popular Sandy Show attracted an entry of 102 exhibits, and was a great success. It was to be the last cat show held in Britain for many a year with the 1939–45 War stopping all such activities. It was thought by many that the Cat Fancy had come to an end, with the veterinary surgeons being sickened by the thousands of cats they had to put down, as families were split up, children evacuated, and men called up. Famous studs were neutered, or put down, breeding queens spayed, and very few people had pedigree kittens for sale. Once the bombing was started, even more cats were put down, or killed by the bombs.

Our own pet, a shorthaired brown tabby, was nearly a victim, as he was in our house when it was completely destroyed by an oil bomb. Fortunately I was away with my children but was heartbroken when I heard what had happened, and gave up the cat as gone. However, about a week after the bombing, Mac, as he was called, was seen by a neighbour to emerge from the ruins. He was taken to the vet, as he had a large bump on his head, to be destroyed, but the vet said he deserved to live, and some days afterwards he was sent to us in an orange box to Sussex where we were staying with an aunt. He lived to a ripe old age.

The War ended and people began to try to live normal lives again. It was hard to believe that there would be no sleeping in the underground and in air raid shelters. Our cat had always been the first to rush to our Anderson shelter when the siren went, followed by the dog and our half a dozen chickens. Many fanciers too always had their cats with them during the air raids, and these and other pedigree cats were to form the nucleus for a much depleted Cat Fancy.

The Notts & Derby Cat Club decided that they would hold the first Cat Show, with Mr A. Jude, the geneticist, as show manager. He said of this show that 'when I was asked to take charge I did so with a full knowledge of the responsibilities ahead. After six abnormal years, the whole aspect of show management was altered, and above all . . . we knew the running costs were infinitely higher.' To everyone's amazement 662 cats and kittens were entered. The Victoria Baths hall was really too small, and to get all the exhibits in some had to be in pens in tiers, one on top of the other. Every precaution was taken, Mr Jude said, with wire netting, roofing felt, and then a covering of white paper to give all the protection needed for the 'ground floor' occupants. The judges had to work hard to get all the exhibits judged, and also to work out which cats had won the 150 specials. Moreover a new ruling by the GCCF meant that cats could no longer be sent by train to be collected by the show managers, and had to be taken to the show hall by the owner or a representative. For this ruling show managers must have heaved sighs of relief. For this show travel was difficult in some cases, and meant cats had to be penned for two nights. All went well on the day, the quality was high, and the gate was good.

Unfortunately the aftermath was disastrous as it was soon realised that 'the scourge is still with us', with many lovely cats and kittens dying. The show ran by the Club the next year attracted a very small entry, with about 150 cats being penned. This may have been because of the death rate the year before.

A small wartime show, of two or three classes, held as a section of a fur and feather show, had been organised by Mrs Brice-Webb at Beeston, Nottingham, and was well supported, so it was natural for the first Championship Show after the war to be held in Nottingham. The Blue Persian Society followed with a show in January 1946, and within the next two years there were eight Championship Shows in London, two in Nottingham, and one in Sandy. The Blue Persians seemed to be as good as ever, and soon new champions were seen on the show benches belonging to pre-war fanciers, such as Mrs Brunton of Dunesk fame and Miss Langston who bred the Allington cats. There were some show reports that said the eyes of the Blues were not the deep copper or orange as they should be. Many of the other varieties were very scarce, particularly the Abyssinians, and the British shorthairs.

Swimming baths became the favourite venues, as at that time they were not open all through the winter as they are today. In 1949 a new variety came to Britain from the USA in the shape of the Burmese. Two cats, Chindwin's Minou Twm and Casa Gatos Foong, had to spend six months in quarantine, and everyone eagerly awaited for them to make their first public appearance. It was said there was a tremendous future for them in Britain. They were already very popular in the States, and in Britain today the Burmese are just as popular as the Siamese.

Unfortunately 1949 saw another outbreak of feline infectious enteritis, as it is now called, and dosing with milk and brandy was recommended. That year the National made a loss of £12 as there was a thick 'pea-souper' that day, and few could even get to the show. Cats had been shown on television, including one of mine, to advertise the show.

Mr Cowlishaw started a monthly magazine *Our Cats* (nothing to do with the original) in 1949 with articles by experts such as Professor J. Haldane on colour breeding. The old question of whether or not cats should be taxed came up again, and Mrs Joan Thompson, the breeder of the famous Pensford cats, wrote a monthly diary, which gave her comments on the shows, details of Annual General Meetings, and described her various judging engagements in most countries of the world. New clubs were being formed all the time, including the Scottish Cat Club, which had vanished well before the war.

A two-day show, the Crystal Cat Show, was held at the Olympia, not under GCCF rules. It proved to be a great success, with about 19,000 people visiting the show. A similar show was held in 1951, sponsored by Chappie, at which a Celebrity Cat of the Year was chosen and received some splendid prizes. It was at the 1950 National that Mrs Joan Thompson's world famous Blue Persian, Champion Gloria of Pensford, ran out of the Paddington Baths when the show was being dismantled, and vanished. The publicity was tremendous, with the newspapers picturing her, and it seemed as if the whole of London was searching for her. It was 41 days before she was found, wet, thin and bedraggled, only a mile from the show hall. She recovered quickly and was soon winning more prizes at other shows.

The 1951 Festival of Britain attracted thousands of visitors to the capital, and a special

cat show had a huge gate. Many people had never been or even heard of a cat show, and there was a great demand for pedigree kittens. The Southern Counties Cat Club ran a most successful show, particularly for me as my kitten, Blue Star George, was best kitten in show. Little did his many admirers at the show realise that I had been up most of the night before trying to make him presentable. I had come the day before to stay with my mother, in order to get to the show early, and George decided to go up the chimney there, and instead of a pale blue Persian kitten a black unrecognisable object came down.

The Governing Council of the Cat Fancy held a special show in 1953 to celebrate the Coronation of Queen Elizabeth. A number of judges from various countries were invited, most of our senior judges took part, and special awards were given. There were 320 cats and kittens,

The All-breed Cat Show, 1952, at the Royal Horticultural Society's New Hall, Westminster.

with very large entries for the Coronation classes.

In 1954 I ran my first National Cat Club show, and little did I think that 30 years later I would still be doing it. The show was held on a Wednesday, and there were 390 exhibits. Surprisingly the gate was good, as nowadays mid-week shows would not be very popular, and all shows are now held on Saturdays.

In the 1950s there was a glimmer of hope that at long last something was being done that could stop the awful death rate after many shows. It was rumoured that in the USA a vaccine was now being used that could immunise cats against feline infectious enteritis, known as FIE for short.

In Britain Borough Wellcome said that they had a vaccine that could be given to kittens at six weeks, but it was imperative that kittens were inoculated as there was no serum that was effective once the infection had taken hold. Some fanciers were against having young kittens inoculated, but others were all for it. One or two kittens did show some form of reaction, but it really did seem that steps were being taken to get rid of the once 'deadly scourge'. Over the years other organisations have also introduced vaccines, and the early ones have been much improved. Today most vaccinations are given when kittens are 9–10 weeks old, some needing only one dose and others two. It is also now a general ruling that no exhibit may enter a GCCF show unless it has a current vaccination certificate supplied by a veterinary surgeon saying that this has been done. A veterinary surgeon will always advise the correct type of vaccine for a specific kitten.

There are also a number of viral respiratory diseases referred to as cat 'flu. There are now several vaccines that will give a kitten some protection against these, but vaccination is not compulsory as yet.

In 1956 the Siamese Cat Club Show was held at the Seymour Hall, Marylebone, London, with 246 cats and kittens entered. Sir Compton

The *News of the World* Pet Cat Class at the National Cat Club Diamond Jubilee Show, Olympia, 1956.

Mackenzie, President of the Club, who loved and wrote about Siamese, came all the way from Scotland to the show.

The Lancs and North Western Counties Cat Club's 1958 Show was spoiled by a blizzard. There were many empty pens, and some that had struggled to get there through the deep snow found that their cats were too late to be judged in their open classes.

I was very pleased at the Surrey and Sussex Cat Club Show at Epsom, when one of my females, Bluestar Sweet Fragrance, was Best Blue adult. She bred many kittens, and any I showed were always prizewinners. She died at the ripe old age of sixteen. The same year I became a delegate to the Governing Council. That year too there was a bus strike which made it very difficult for many members to get to the Blue Persian Cat Society's AGM in May.

In 1956 there were pet cat classes at the National for the first time. This followed many months of discussion, for some of the committee thought it was not quite the thing to have mongrel cats and kittens at the Premier Cat Club's pedigree show. A friend of mine, Brian Vesey-Fitzgerald, the well-known writer on animals, thought it an excellent idea and agreed to judge some pets for us. At that time, he was writing an animal column for the *News of the World*, and they agreed to sponsor the classes, not to give us money, but to offer a trophy for the Best Pet Feline. The first year we had about 190 pets in addition to 500 pedigree cats. The showing of pets really was a success, and ever since then we have had pet cats, and many other clubs now have pet sections as well.

The club felt that pet classes would encourage children and adults to look after and groom their cats, which it has done. Many of the original young exhibitors now have children of their own, who show their pets; others have become well-known pedigree breeders; and some are now judges.

Pet cats do help the publicity for a show, as

The first *Blue Peter* cat Jason, at the National Cat Club Show.

the national press give more space to pets than they do to the pedigree. A whole family will come to the show just to bring their pet, and friends and neighbours will often come just to see how the cats fared.

In 1964 while I was up at the BBC studios I happened to mention the pet classes and how many entries we received from children, and that it seemed to be encouraging them to look after the cats properly. Biddy Baxter, the editor of *Blue Peter*, thought it would be a good idea to put on special classes for *Blue Peter* viewers, and in 1965 this happened. The response was terrific, with van loads of mail arriving from viewers wanting to show their pets. Of course, not all of them did, as we had over 900 pedigrees and could only have about 200 pets that first year. Johnny Morris and Valerie Singleton were among the pet cat judges, and the section was managed by my sister, Mrs Walde. Mrs Menezes brought along Jason, the *Blue Peter* cat, and there were long queues all day long to see him. When he died Jack and Jill came, and we have had them each year. Unfortunately Jill died recently, but Jack still comes. We have one of the *Blue Peter* team to judge the winners that go on the actual programme, with the team choosing the Best *Blue Peter* champion. In 1966 there were 460 pets entered, and for many years we have had a ballot to choose the viewers' cats that may be entered, so popular have they become.

At one show Independent Television asked if they could televise the show live. After much discussion the committee agreed. I was taken aback when they worked out their programme minute by minute, as at a cat show it is really almost impossible to keep to a strict time for a judge to be handling a specific cat or kitten. We did our best, however, and the programme did attract countrywide interest from viewers who had never realised up to then that there were such things as cat shows.

Since those days we have had both the BBC and ITV at many shows, usually taping programmes to be shown later, and these have really delighted many viewers. There was controversy over the televising of the judging for the Best in Show, as it was said that the lights upset the cats, making them sometimes difficult to handle. In most cases now it has been stopped. In any case not all shows have Best in Show, but Best of Breed, that is the best cat or kitten or each variety. All in all, television has given valuable publicity to cat shows over the years.

The 1960s and 70s saw a great increase in the number of clubs and the number of shows. In 1901 there were 27 breeds seen at the shows; today there are over 100 possible colours and coat patterns recognised. This means many more classes at the shows, as an open class must be provided for each variety. Cats that come under the heading of 'Any Other Colour or Variety' have up until recently been shown in assessment classes only. Now they may also enter miscellaneous classes as well with other cats.

There are over 80 affiliated clubs that are entitled to send delegates to the GCCF, which amounts to about 150 attending each council meeting.

Cats that have no provisional standard can only be shown on exhibition, as was the case when the first Turkish cats were imported from that country. They differed from the early Angoras in that they had some red markings on their white coats. The first time they appeared at a show the national press heard about their reputation for swimming in warm pools and shallow rivers in Turkey. One newspaper telephoned me to ask at what times during the day the cats would be giving their swimming demonstrations, as they wished to send a photographer along!

Many new varieties were being exhibited, some produced by selective breeding, such as the Colourpoints (Himalayan in the States), the Rex by mutation, the Burmese by imports, and so on.

In 1971 the National Cat Club held a special show to celebrate a Centenary of Cat Shows, issuing a souvenir catalogue giving the history of the Cat Fancy, and inviting judges from the United States and Europe to judge alongside the British judges.

CENTENARY OF CAT SHOWS
CRYSTAL PALACE 1871 — OLYMPIA 1971

THE
NATIONAL CAT CLUB
75th CHAMPIONSHIP CAT SHOW

WITH ACKNOWLEDGEMENTS
TO OUR CATS DECEMBER 1912

**CATALOGUE
40p**

In 1976 The Governing Council decided to start running a show of their own, called the Supreme. They had run one years before, but this was to be different in that the cats and kittens had to qualify by winning their open classes at shows during the year. Special awards to count towards championships were given, and cups were given for the Supreme Best Adult, Kitten and Neuter, with a Best being chosen between the Adult and the Kitten. There were also cups for the best in each section, i.e. Longhair, British Shorthair, Foreign Shorthair, and Siamese cats, kittens and neuters. The show got off to a slow start at first, as it took some fanciers quite a time to get used to the idea of a show that was different. However, the entries have gradually increased over the years. There is now a section for pet cats, and, as with the National when they first had pet cat classes, there were many who did not approve, but the GCCF realised that pets do help the publicity. It is also possible to have celebrities judging them which helps to bring in the public. The 1983 Supreme Show was the most successful yet, which is a good omen for the 1985 show. This is to be a special one with overseas judges as well as British to celebrate the 75th birthday of the Governing Council of the Cat Fancy.

The 1980s have seen a slight falling-off of some of the entries at the shows, but this is probably due to the general situation in the country, and doubtless the Cat Fancy, the clubs, the shows and above all the cats will go on increasing over the years.

Opposite: The cover of the centenary catalogue.

4 The Development of Cat Shows Worldwide

USA

The success of the Crystal Palace show and the interest in pedigree cats that followed, with its repercussions throughout the Cat Fancy, seemed to have made a great impression in the United States. There had already been cat shows held in North America, although not everyone realised it. These were shows for the Coon cats in Maine.

Maine was one of the largest shipbuilding States, with constant arrivals and departures of ships from all parts of the world. Seafaring men would often return home with kittens as pets for their wives and children. Frequently these kittens had long fur and came from the East, and eventually they mated with the resident domestic shorthaired cats. This produced massive hardy cats, with longish silky coats, very dense, probably because of the severe winters in Maine. The majority were brown tabbies, with white chests, with markings that resembled those of the racoons. It was thought that they were the progeny of cats and racoons mating, as it was not then realised that this was biologically impossible. For many years shows were held to choose the best Maine cats.

The kittens were so attractive that frequently they were taken by visitors to other parts of the States, and it was realised that the Coons were in danger of disappearing from Maine. Some fanciers did their best to keep the variety going, but more and more pedigree cats were being imported from Britain, and interest in the Coon cats grew less and less, until by 1904 they had almost disappeared from the shows. A few fanciers kept them going over the years, and in 1953 the Central Maine Cat Club was formed, and once again a show was held. In 1968 the Maine Coon Breeders and Fanciers Association

was formed to promote the interest and breeding of the Maine Coon cats. They succeeded so well that today they have their official standard, are recognised in many colours, have Championship status, and have also been exported to Europe.

In 1883 a 'Grand Cat Show' was held in Boston, which was organised by the Boston Cat Club, and ran for two weeks. According to the *Boston Traveller*, the local newspaper, published on October 16, 'there were heavy cats, thin cats, old cats, Angora cats, Siberian cats, Coon cats, Maltese cats and Tiger cats . . . about 400 of them, with crowds waiting for the 10 o'clock opening.'

The cats were arranged according to colour, curiosities, cross-eyed, three-legged and long-tailed cats, Maltese, Angora cats and kittens. Another paper, *The Globe*, wrote that a Manx named Jumbo and a five-legged pet were the main attractions. The winners were awarded gold and silver medals, silver collars, and many other prizes, together with money totalling 500 dollars.

In 1895, Mr J.T. Hyde, an Englishman, who had visited the Crystal Palace show, decided to run a cat show on the same lines in the Madison Square Garden, New York, on May 8. Mr Hyde had previously been involved with horse shows in that venue. Dr Huidekoper, Miss Hurlburt and Mr T. Farrer Rackham were the judges. Included in the show were eight cats from England, but several died shortly afterwards. The show was a huge success, although it was a very hot day with temperatures up in the 90s Fahrenheit which was hard upon the cats. The surprise Best in Show was a Brown Tabby, one of the cats from Maine. A fancier said she came

The Empire Show, Pier Terminal, New York – the US Cat Fanciers' Association's oldest club.

from Maine and, 'her cats were not Coon cats, as there were others there as well as Coons.'

A further show was held in the autumn at Newburgh, on the Hudson River, and another was arranged for 1896, with one being held in New York in between. The second one in New York was much better arranged, and there were more varieties and colours shown. Some fanciers met at the show and decided to form a club to be known as the National, but it seemed to fade away, as nothing further was heard of it. It was five years before another cat show was held in New York, and this was in the Concert Hall in Madison Square, with an entry of 110 cats.

A show was held in Chicago in 1898, three years after the New York show, and was such a success that it was decided to form the Chicago Cat Club, which attracted many members and did well, until another club was formed. This was the Beresford Cat Club, named after the English cat breeder, Lady Marcus Beresford, which very soon completely overshadowed the Chicago Club. Before long it had 300 members and the Club's show in Chicago attracted an entry of 250 cats. The second show held by the Club under the auspices of the National Fanciers Association of Chicago, on January 21 1901, ran for four days. The entry was over 200, and it was reported that the quality and style of the longhairs was much improved from last year. Apparently the shorthairs were numerous and tried the physical powers of the judge, a Mrs C. McCloud. The writer of the report on the show was a Mrs Locke, the owner of the Lockehaven cattery, who with her husband exhibited 26 cats and kittens. The Best Longhaired Cat in Show was Melrose Lassie, a cat from England, said to be the best blue longhaired in America. Mr Locke showed and won with a number of cats, but the writer Mrs Locke said that: 'It goes without saying that Mr Locke, who has spent more money, and given more time to breeding and purchasing, must have naturally won the greatest number of prizes, and though in some instances the classes only contained one or two. The judges did not award 1st and 2nd prizes unless deserved.'

Another winning cat sent over from England was an outstanding Black, Blackberry Fawe. The Orange (now Red) cats did well, with one The Prince of Orange being unbeaten. The best meat from Armours was served to the cats, and each one had a red cushion on a shelf in the cage, with earth being used in the litter trays and changed each day.

A later report on the show said that although the crowd was impressive, and everything seemed a brilliant success, the show lost money. Apparently the Coliseum, where the show was held, charged 500 dollars a day and evening for the rent, and everything else was just as expensive. The writer went on to ask whether English Cat Shows were ever remunerative.

Shows were gradually being held all over the country, with imports from Britain continuing. This apparently worried the US Government, as it appeared that they were losing revenue with the number of cats coming into the country free of duty. In 1902 they made a law as follows:

When one wishes to bring a feline into the United States free of duty, he must be able to produce a pedigree of sufficient dignity to satisfy the officials of the Government having authority under the Tariff Law to prescribe the conditions under which pure bred animals may be imported into the United States free of customs duty. Moreover the pedigree must be accompanied by the affidavit of the importer, and also a certificate of registration in the only stud book recognised by the Government as eligible to enforce these requirements.

The duty payable was 20 per cent of the cat's value.

To make things even more difficult for the importer, as apparently the system for making a

The busy scene at an American show.

cat a champion differed in the two countries, a further notice appeared:

The United States Official Register Association announces that the Registrar of its stud book has been directed not to recognise any championships until such times as the Championship rules of England and America come sufficiently into accord for winnings in one country to carry with them honours equal to those of another. It is intended to record in the stud book merely the names of cats eligible for free entrance into the U.S.A. Their pedigrees and other evidence of qualification for acceptance will appear in the Register.

One fancier (a lady) wrote and complained that everything went well in the USA Cat Fancy until gentlemen decided to get involved! Apparently a committee was set up for proving pedigrees, which must have been very difficult for it was common practice both in England and America to change a cat's name when it was sold from one person to another.

There was no quarantine and cats could be sent to the States and after winning could go back to England, but this rarely happened.

The Deep South was very interested in cats and several fanciers started to breed kittens, but apparently found it 'impossible because of the fleas', and had to give up.

A show held in 1903 by the Atlantic Cat Club, which had a number of wealthy members, was a great success, with many cups and specials being given. Mr Farrar Rackham, who had judged at the first show in New York, was responsible for that and a number of very successful shows in Boston. In California too there were many shows, with English cats or their progeny invariably winning.

Unfortunately the cats and kittens at the shows were now affected in the same way as in Britain with many dying after being exhibited. So heavy was the loss of life following a show held in New York in 1904 that an enquiry was started to find out the cause, and a full investigation was ordered. The show was a two-day one, and it made no difference as to whether the animals were taken home or left in the hall all night. There was evidence that one cat had been taken ill at the show and was sent home to die two days later. An autopsy was carried out on as many of the bodies as possible. Obviously we know now that the deaths were caused by a very virulent form of feline infectious enteritis, but one expert said that it was cholera, or distemper. Another blamed worming immediately after the show, as apparently was often done. It was also said that the weather in New York was extra cold and the hall heating was turned on so high that exhibitors had to take their coats off, and the cats 'took cold' through being too hot. It is pitiful now to read some experts' reports and to know that it was realised that it was a virus that spread rapidly, but even going as far as that there was no known cure.

Fanciers were told to let their cats live as much an outdoor life as possible, not to keep

Setting up the show at midnight – the River City Cat Show, Texas.

them too hot, and to worm before and not after a show, and to make sure they were not constipated. Cascara was recommended the day before the show. There seemed to be no suggestion that it would be better not to exhibit at all, and still the same fanciers who had already lost animals continued to enter.

As of now, English judges were occasionally invited to judge, and when Louis Wain, President and Chairman of the National Cat Club, went to work for the *New York American*, one of the Randolph Hearst newspapers, he was welcomed as a judge that could always be relied on. He stayed in the States from 1907 to 1910. At one show to everyone's surprise, as there were comparatively few Siamese, he made one Best in Show. Fanciers were finding Siamese very difficult to breed, with the warmth in California seeming to suit them better than elsewhere in the States. At the shows there were more shown than at others throughout the country.

The American Cat Association was founded in 1901, registering and sponsoring shows throughout the continent. 1906 saw the founding of the Cat Fanciers Association, which also began registering cats and sponsoring shows. Over the years it grew to be the largest association, as more and more clubs were formed and were taken under the CFA's wing. It also has affiliated clubs in Japan, which has a lively Cat Fancy, with many American judges officiating at the shows there, as well as their own judges.

Japan has a number of cat clubs, such as the Japan International Cat Fanciers, and the Cat Fanciers of Osaka. Many of their cats have come from the States, pedigree of course, but in an old magazine in 1901 a shipment of 4,000 cats was cleared at Washington to go to Japan. A further 10,000 cats were also required to help destroy the rat plague which was rapidly spreading throughout the country.

In the States, a Mr C.H. Jones, one of the early cat fanciers, decided that interest in cats was growing all the time, and started to publish the *Cat Journal*, a monthly magazine, which did a great deal to promote breeding and showing for many years, and really helped the growth of the American Cat Fancy.

Before long, as in England, many wealthy people were owning large catteries, having staff to look after them; and, although distances between the shows were very great, this enabled some fanciers to travel to shows in various parts of the country.

The coming of the motor car, and much later the aeroplane, was responsible for the great growth of shows and cats, until today America has far more pedigree cats than any other country in the world.

CANADA

In the beginning Canada cat fanciers were very involved, and still are, with the Cat Fancy in the USA registering their cats with the various associations there, and exhibiting frequently. The first recorded show in Canada was in 1906 when the Royal Canadian Cat Club organised a show which attracted 192 entries. It lasted two days and was held in Toronto. It was said that the majority of cats shown were of unknown pedigree, but there were some beautiful Persians of various colours, including Blue, Black, Silver and Orange. The Siamese did not appear at the shows for a number of years.

There is a story of one of the early imports from Britain in 1904 (unfortunately it does not say which variety, but it was probably a longhair), which a Mrs Burns took back to Canada with her. She wrote that 'on the steamer he had a cabin to himself in the sailors' quarters. He did not seem to mind that voyage at all, although it was exceedingly rough.' On arrival he had to travel in the luggage van, and while the train was in a siding at night the man went to feed him, whereupon he jumped out of his basket and out into the night. Luckily it was only a small village where he escaped, and he was found after two days in the wilderness none the worse for his adventure, and was sent on to his new home by train. His name was Cairo Ramadan and he had belonged to a Mrs Clarke. I have tried to trace him without success in the National Cat Club Stud book for 1900–1905, so possibly he was never shown in Britain, or even registered.

The Victoria Cat Club held a two-day show in March 1912, with some splendid cats being exhibited. Among the winners was Ch. Silver Troughton, belonging to a Mrs Troughton, and

Opposite: Two top American cats, from *Our Cats*, September 1959.

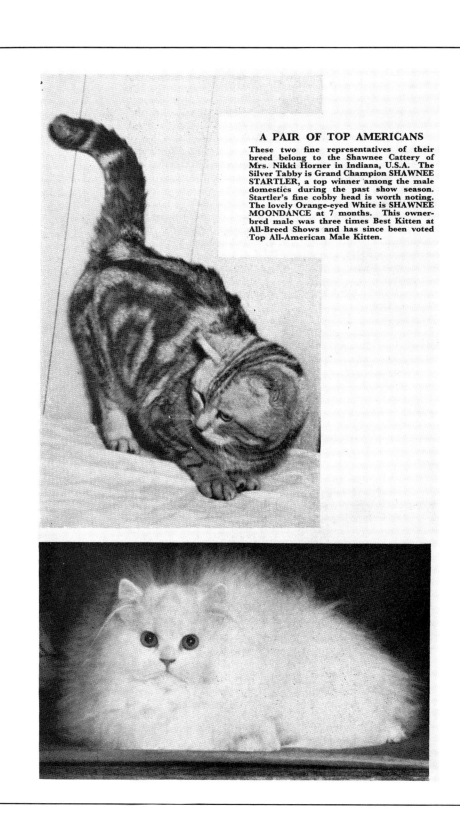

A PAIR OF TOP AMERICANS

These two fine representatives of their breed belong to the Shawnee Cattery of Mrs. Nikki Horner in Indiana, U.S.A. The Silver Tabby is Grand Champion SHAWNEE STARTLER, a top winner among the male domestics during the past show season. Startler's fine cobby head is worth noting. The lovely Orange-eyed White is SHAWNEE MOONDANCE at 7 months. This owner-bred male was three times Best Kitten at All-Breed Shows and has since been voted Top All-American Male Kitten.

Bindi, an orange and white owned by Mrs Rathbone. Neither of these cats appear in the British stud book and register, but it is possible that the name was altered by the new owners. The heaviest cat in show was a blue neuter by Crystal Palace Bob and Ch. Doreen, very well known cats in Britain, so the cat must have been imported. He was shown by a Mrs Elliott. Vancouver also held a show in August 1912, and there was one in Toronto in December the same year.

One or two Siamese were imported, but longhairs seemed to have been most favoured. Both of the world wars had a devastating effect on the Canadian Cat Fancy, but fanciers continued to show at local shows and also travelled far afield to the United States, having registered their cats there.

After the 1939–45 War the Canadian National Cat Club, one of the oldest clubs, was again responsible for annual shows at the Canadian National Exhibition, where many varieties of animals were also shown. The show attracted exhibitors from all over the States and Canada.

In 1960, the Canadian Cat Association was formed, the first registering body in the country, with the first show being held in Ottawa in 1963. More clubs came into existence, and soon were sponsoring shows. Some clubs were affiliated with the American Associations. Many of the Canadian-bred cats were soon winning in the large American shows, and there was great demand for the kittens.

In 1968, the Canadian National Cat Club was disbanded and the cat section of the Canadian National Exhibition was held under the sponsorship of the Royal Canadian Cat Club.

The shows are run under similar lines to those in the States, with similar classes. In addition to the Championships and Grand Championships offered, it is also possible to make a cat an International Grand Champion by winning at both Canadian and American shows.

The Canadian Cat Fancy is now one of the biggest, with every variety being exhibited and bred throughout the country, and kittens being eagerly sought by fanciers throughout the whole continent.

AUSTRALIA AND NEW ZEALAND

Australia has no native domestic cats, although there was a so-called Australian cat shown in America at the end of the last century; but this was said to have resulted from a Siamese from Britain cross-breeding with a cat in Australia, and the offspring being sent to America. The Australia Cat Fancy was slow in starting, as distance was a great problem, and cats had to come by ship from Britain, which took five or six weeks, or from New Zealand. There was no quarantine from Britain at first, but it was reported in 1901 that 'the laws regarding quarantine are now carried out so stringently in New Zealand so as to make exporting or importing animals a tedious and difficult matter.' Things are easier now, as quite a few cats are imported into Australia from New Zealand, and many win at the shows.

In 1901 The Great Annual Show of the Victoria Poultry and Kennel Club was held in Melbourne on July 19 and 20. There were 21 classes in all, including Persians, Siamese, Manx, Striped Tabbies, Spotted Tabbies, Black and White, Tortie and White, Any Other Variety, Heaviest Cat, Best Pair of Kittens. The entry fee was 1s.6d. a class.

A further report about cats in Australia said there were some cats, but they were funny little beasts, sitting up like squirrels, with much the same shape of head, very quaint, and did not live long. They sound more like marmots than cats.

At first most of the cats imported were longhairs of various colours, Dr Roper sending two very good Blacks from Britain, and another breeder sent a Blue champion called Waverley. Mrs King of Scone imported two Silver Tabbies, Darby and Joan, which were responsible for a number of kittens which were sent all over the continent. Darby unfortunately died in 1903, but Silver Tabbies by then were well established. In 1906, Miss Simpson sent her blue stud, Blue Beau, which in spite of the extra long sea voyage arrived in 'very good order'. In Victoria Mrs M'Lennan of Moonee Ponds had Persians of all colours, and also the very rare

Royal Siamese. Breeders found that the demand for kittens both in New South Wales and Victoria was good, with kittens selling from £3 3s. These cats and many others were to form the foundation for the very lively Cat Fancy in Australia today.

Cat Clubs were formed, but over the early years most faded away. In 1919 a Club was formed which still functions today. Of all the States, Victoria and New South Wales were the most cat-minded, and in 1928 the Governing Council of the Cat Fancy of Australia was founded in Victoria. It was hoped that this Council would be the only registering body, but this proved impractical. The Cat Fancies spread slowly through the various States, but struggled on to survive during the war years. It was impossible then to import any more cats from Britain; but dedicated breeders managed to keep the interest in pedigree cats going.

The 1950s saw a revival with cats and kittens being sent over once again from Britain and New Zealand. More registering bodies came into being, with some of the States having more than one. Many new clubs were formed, and became affiliated to the relevant registering Council, and soon shows were being held in nearly every state, some clubs holding two shows a year.

In such a large country it would be difficult to have one registering body. The seven States, Northern Territory, Queensland, South Australia, West Australia, Victoria and New South Wales, and the island of Tasmania, each have their own Governing Councils, with many of the shows being held under the auspices of the Royal Agricultural Society. Each State has a number of clubs, which run shows, some holding two a year. There is a Co-ordinating Council of Australia which seeks to do that between the various Cat Fancies.

Shows are run under their own controlling body, but the rules are very much the same, as is the system of judging. One or two of the clubs are trying ring judging, but the majority prefer the same method as used in Britain of going to the cages with a steward.

There is an interchange of judges between the separate States, and all judges have to attend

The Best British Blue at the Mersey Show, Tasmania, 1982.

training courses and sit examinations. Judges from overseas are frequently invited to judge, with the very high costs being borne by a number of clubs.

At the shows there are open classes for each variety, but the Best in Show is chosen by the panel of judges going separately to the cats nominated in their pens. This is done at a few shows in Britain. Some have classes for kittens under three months; Tasmanian or Australian bred, Interstate bred, best eye colour, best type, also personality and best-groomed classes, all of which attracted good entries. Other classes are similar to those at the British cat shows, and there is usually a section for pet cats. Many trophies, ribbons and rosettes are given.

The distances in Australia are so vast that local shows tend to have entries of about 300 cats, but the show held annually in Sydney may have more than 1,000 exhibits. Air travel has helped, but it does make showing and breeding expensive, as cats may have to be flown thousands of miles if the services of a particular male are required. Judges too may have to fly long distances from the north to the south just for a one-day show. The Central Australian Cat Club holds three shows a year, but as the shows are held in Alice Springs right in the centre of Australia the average entry is about 40 cats, which fully justifies the claim that their shows are the smallest in the continent.

With the climatic variations it is possible to hold shows all the year round. I had not realised how much the coats of the longhairs could vary according to the area from which they came until I judged there. I had always thought of Australia as the land of sunshine and warmth. It was quite a shock to find on the morning of the Canberra show that the car had to be de-iced before we could go, but the longhairs I judged had beautiful luxurious coats, so the climate obviously suited them.

Tasmania has a flourishing Cat Fancy, with a number of shows being held every year, with the clubs being affiliated with the Cat Control Council of Tasmania, and the shows conducted under the auspices of the Royal Agricultural Society of Tasmania.

Although the island has its own Cat Fancy, there is no sense of isolation from the mainland, and there are many cats imported from Britain, New Zealand, and other parts of Australia. I judged for the Launceston (All Breeds) Cat Club, which had had its first Championship show in 1967, with an entry of about 120 exhibits. When I judged there in 1976 there were nearly 300 exhibits, and practically every recognised variety was well represented.

The Cat Fancy in New Zealand is under the control of the New Zealand Cat Fancy, until recently known as the Governing Council of the Cat Fancy of New Zealand. The country is divided into three regions, with 36 member clubs. Each region sends a representative to the thrice-yearly regional meetings. They elect there a Chairman and Vice-chairman to attend the National Executive, which hold meetings three times a year. Representatives from all the clubs attend an Annual General Meeting, and any major decisions made there are put forward to the National Executive.

It is a very lively and active Cat Fancy, which started some years ago with imports from Britain, mostly longhairs at that time. Judges' training courses and seminars are held frequently. The majority of the clubs hold at least one Championship show a year, under National Show rules. A few shows have ring judging now, but up until now judging has been as in Britain with the judges and stewards going to the pens.

Many fanciers have gone in for selective and careful breeding programmes, with the result that many outstanding cats may be seen at the shows, where most varieties are well represented. There are no quarantine restrictions for cats sent from Australia and vice versa, and a number are flown across the Tasman Sea to introduce new blood into both countries.

There is a strange story about the origin of the shorthaired blue cats in New Zealand. It is said that in 1850 a small French colony came and settled in the Akaroa Peninsula, bringing with them a number of shorthaired blue cats. Immediately this news reached British ears, a man-of-war was sent to plant the Union Jack in that Territory. Apparently the French fled in haste, so quickly that all the cats were left behind. The cats bred well, and at the beginning of the twentieth century it was said that no fashionable lady in Christchurch would be without one. These cats were probably the ancestors of the various shorthairs seen in New Zealand today.

SOUTH AFRICA

Egypt is considered to have been the birthplace of the domestic cat several thousands of years ago, but there is very little known about other cats in the continent of Africa. South Africa seems to have been the only State to have shown much interest in pedigree cats in the early days of the Cat Fancy, and it is known that visitors to Britain did take cats back to South Africa with them.

In 1900 a Dr and Mrs Abbot, who had lived out there, brought their cats back with them; one was Peter, whose father was a Persian and mother a Cape Cat. They also had a Smoke but this had come from America. In a 1904 issue of

Our Cats there is a pathetic letter about a Mrs Donovan who lived in Natal, saying that 'during the horrors of the Boer War all her pure-bred Persian cats came to an untimely end.' She asked for a catalogue of the Crystal Palace show as she was anxious to have at least one cat to replace them, and wanted one to be sent out by ship. A cat called Lord Roberts did go to South Africa, but whether it was sent to Mrs Donovan or not I cannot trace. In 1901, Blue Boy III, an outstanding prizewinner, was sent to the Cape to be a mate for a daughter of Darius, another famous Blue.

The South African Cat Union was founded in 1946, but there did not appear to be any clubs then. It was later that the Western Province Cat Club in Cape Town came into being and was affiliated to the Union. There was very little progress in the Cat Fancy until 1949, when a few Siamese owners got together to discuss their cats and to hold shows. Clubs were formed in Cape Town, Durban and Johannesburg, with well laid down constitutions and show rules. These were similar to the GCCF in Britain, with some amendments to suit conditions in South Africa. Eventually the Associated Cat Club of South Africa was formed, consisting of the Western Province Cat Club, in Cape Town, The Natal Cat Club in Durban, the Rand Cat Club and the Siamese Cat Society in Johannesburg. The four clubs held an annual show and breeders and fanciers took their cats by road or air to each other's show. In Cape Town, the Eastern Province Cat Club was founded, and also the All Breeds Cat Club.

The interest grew rapidly and the Governing Council of the Cat Fancy of South Africa came into being, the only liaison body between the clubs, with one delegate per club meeting as required, usually annually, to discuss any relevant matters. The clubs are run individually, controlled only by the show rules, which are similar to those in Britain. Recently another Club was formed in the Transvaal, the Cat Fanciers' Club, so there are now seven clubs and thirteen shows being held each year. Awards given at each show are recognised by other clubs, provided that accredited judges officiate at these functions.

There are no mixed breeds classes, as in Britain, other than the Supreme or Grand Challenge classes. Judging the Grand Challenge classes is usually done by two judges using the points system, and a definite number of points must be awarded before a certificate can be given. This applies too to the Supreme classes, with possibly three judges being involved. As in Britain a current FIE certificate must be held before an exhibit may be shown, but this applies only up to the age of three years. Males too can only be shown provided a vet has certified that the male is entire, and only kittens from a registered stud male can be registered.

The Standard of Points in use is based on the GCCF standards, and may be amended to suit local conditions. Any decisions regarding the Standards and show rules are discussed by three judges' panels, with any changes agreed to being passed to the Governing Council to send to the clubs for approval, and acceptance, if agreed.

The distances are so great between the various clubs that few cats are shown outside of their own province. Judges, however, do travel from one part of the country to another to judge at shows. Because of the heat judging starts at 8.30 am and is usually finished by lunchtime. The judges and stewards go to the pens with their trolleys. The judges confer to choose the Best in Show.

In South Africa, the Siamese Cat Society, which has always catered for all breeds, has now changed its name to the Transvaal Cat Society, a very suitable title for the first Society formed in the Transvaal.

ZIMBABWE

The Cat Fancy in Zimbabwe has suffered over the past few years, due to the change in the country. It has become very difficult to import new stock, and the migration of breeders has reduced the numbers of both cats and exhibitors, which seems likely to continue. South Africa has benefited from this, with breeders from Zimbabwe tending to settle in the larger areas. Natal and the Transvaal now have new exhibitors and new pedigree blood lines, although many of the original cats came from South Africa.

There are two clubs in the country, one in Bulawayo and the other in Harare. They meet to try to keep breeders in touch and also to hold very small shows. Some of the judges have left, but they do try to have a South African judge from time to time. The faithful few battle on, but owing to the difficulty of sending money out of the country it is almost impossible to get new stock.

EUROPE

The first longhairs seen in Britain came from France, but the history of the shorthairs is much the same throughout Europe, with the resident domestic cats mating with other cats introduced there by travellers and seafaring men. The Chartreuse, a shorthaired Blue, very similar to the British Blue, was brought to France from South Africa by the Chartreuse monks, who bred them for many years.

The first cat show in Paris was in the 1890s, and was held in the Jardin d'Acclimatation in Paris. It became an annual event and the fifth held in 1901 was a great success, with 256 cats being exhibited, of which 37 were Siamese. One prize was £12, and there were others of £6, £4 and £2. A gold medal offered by the Directors of the Jardin was won by a dwarf cat from Asia, a variety which had never been seen at an English show. It was fully-grown but only the size of a kitten. Strangely enough some years ago in England midget cats were being exhibited which received a great deal of attention, but they only seemed to live for about two years, and the breeding was not carried on.

France was closely associated with Britain for many years, with British judges officiating at the shows, as they still do today. A number of cats were imported from Britain, and in 1927 the Cat Club de Paris held its first show. Another club, La Société Central Feline de France, came into being, but in 1933 the two clubs amalgamated, as the Cat Fancy gradually expanded, but everything ceased with the coming of war

in 1939. All the cat pens were lost during the German occupation, but somehow in 1946 the Club managed to put on a show. A number of new clubs came into existence, and eventually were affiliated with the Fédération Internationale Féline d'Europe now known as FIFE. Many other cat clubs throughout Europe are also associated with the Federation. Other clubs were also founded, including Les Amis du Chats, Cercle Félin de Paris, and a number of others, which do not come under FIFE, and are referred to as the Independents.

Most countries in Europe now have cat shows, including Germany, Austria, Belgium, Czechoslovakia, Denmark, Finland, France, Holland, Italy, Norway, Hungary, Sweden, San Marino, and Switzerland. Most shows are for two days. Some follow the same method of judging as Britain, with judges and stewards going to the pens, and others have the judges in a separate room or a partitioned part of the show hall, with the stewards bringing the cats for judging. In the latter case, all the pens may be decorated with curtains, cushions and maybe flowers, and the hall looks very festive, especially as some exhibitors display all the previously-won rosettes. Rarely are money prizes awarded, the prize-winners receiving rosettes, ribbons, certificates and possibly gifts.

There are no side classes, but there are classes for International Champions and Premiers, Champion of Champions of each variety, with separate classes for males and females. The award is known as CACIB (Certificat d'Apitude de Championnat International de Beauté). The class for Premiers has CAPIB given to the first prize-winner.

The open class is for cats over ten months old, with each breed having classes for male and female. The award given is the CAC (Certificat d'Apitude de Championnat). Neuters too have their own classes, with CAP (Certificat d'Apitude de Premium) being given to the first prize-winners. Kittens have their own classes for each variety, 3–6 months and 6–10 months. There are also classes for neutered kittens and litters. All exhibits must be registered with the appropriate Association. Each cat is given a qualification thought worthy of it; that is Excellent, Very Good, Good or Fairly Good.

The various countries' shows are very similar, and the Cat Fancies appear to be expanding all the time.

Norway had an exhibition in 1933, which included racoons, foxes, household cats and other pets, which attracted a great deal of attention. The first Club was known as the Club of Friends of the Cat, which held one of the first shows. In 1938 The Norse Rasekatt Klub was formed, and the Club of Friends was wound up. With the coming of war, there were no more shows, but in 1945 they started up again by the organisation known as Norak, which is affiliated to FIFE. Many of the cats and kittens seen at the shows have British ancestry. The Antwerp Cat Club in Belgium is thought to be the oldest Cat Club in Europe, having been formed over 70 years ago. It ran shows for many years and then stopped for a few years, but it now seems to be doing well again. There are other shows in Belgium both for FIFE and the Independents, with the standard of exhibits being high. British judges officiate regularly.

The Dutch Cat Club de Nederlands organised a show at the Hague in February 1950, and the best cats all came from England. There are many shows held annually throughout Holland, some very large, and one or two also include other pets, such as rabbits, and guinea pigs. The presentation there is usually very good, with the halls looking most attractive.

Denmark held one of the earliest cat shows in Europe in 1901, with one held in the Royal Zoological Gardens in Copenhagen organised by the Director. To increase the number entered they had suggested that cats might be sent from all other countries travelling on the Parkeston–Esbjerg route, and arrangements could be made for them to be sold at the show. In the report of the show this is not mentioned at all, although they had offered to pay all the cats' fares. There was a class for Angora cats, Siamese, and one for pure-bred cats of different sorts, with the fourth and largest class for Danish domestic cats, including Ratcats. Plates and diplomas were given as prizes, with a special one for a light grey and striped Cyprus cat. The Zoological Gardens Society exhibited a collection of cats, so that people could realise what a good classification there was. They included Abyssinians, Siamese, Fairies (?), tail-less cats from the Isle of Man, and pure-bred cats. There were 200 exhibits.

Germany seems to have come into the Cat Fancy in the early 1920s, with a show organised by Herr K. Hirschmann in Nuremberg, with Angora cats, domestic cats and two Siamese Temple cats wearing gold-plated collars, the first seen in Germany. In 1922 the first stud book was started. Shows were held in Frankfurt, Berlin, Dresden and Rheims. Birmans were appearing there in the 1930s. Everything ceased with the war, but started up again in 1952, with the first show for twelve years. Imports from Britain included a number of longhairs and Siamese, and helped the Cat Fancy to start up again. A number of shows are held throughout the years by the various clubs both for FIFE and the Independents, with British judges often taking part.

The Svenska Kattlubben in Sweden held their first show in Stockholm in 1946, with several English judges. The Cat Fancy there has flourished steadily over the years, with many shows being held under FIFE and other organisations. The standard of the cats shown is very high, with most varieties being exhibited.

Switzerland became interested in pedigree cats through French breeders, and the First International Show was held in Geneva in 1933. This attracted a great deal of attention from all parts of the country, and led to the formation of the Association of the Cat-lovers of Zurich. This club ran a show in 1934 and included there were very dark Red Tabbies from Germany, and an outstanding Cream male from England, Mick of Bredon. Persians became very popular, but Siamese were very few. A number of Clubs and Societies were formed, including during the war the Société Suisse du Chat Persan et Simmois, founded by Madame Gibbons and her sister. The former was a well-known breeder and cat judge, having judged in Britain. They had come from France to get away from the war, and brought all their cats with them, which helped the Swiss breeding considerably. No shows were being held, but after the War they began to be organised by the various clubs.

In Finland, the Suomen Rotukissayhoistyr r.y. (Surok), founded over twenty years ago, began to hold shows under FIFE, with both shorthairs, Siamese and Abyssinians, and a number of Persians being entered. A number of cats have been imported to help the breeding, and the standard seems to be high.

In Czechoslovakia, at the 1980 Prague show there were over 400 cats, with longhairs being the most popular.

Shows have been held a number of times in Vienna, in Austria, and in Budapest in Hungary, where they attract a very good gate. In fact when I judged there people were queuing all day long. Italy and San Marino have one or two cat clubs, hold shows, and British judges have been asked several times. It is possible for breeders to travel to most countries in Europe

and Scandinavia, and by winning at various shows can make their cats International Champions or International Premiers, which because of the quarantine regulations is not possible for British fanciers.

Both Northern and Southern Ireland have several cat clubs, with Northern Ireland being under the jurisdiction of the GCCF, and the South having their own Council as a separate country. Endeavours are now being made by the British GCCF to alter our regulations so that it is possible for the Irish to exhibit in Northern Ireland.

British judges frequently go to Belfast to judge at the several shows held there and other parts of Northern Ireland. Many cats have been imported from Britain and America, and there are some outstanding cats seen at the shows.

In Dublin the shows attract a good gate, and include a number of cats from Britain, but there are also breeders in Southern Ireland producing very good stock.

5 The Pedigree Varieties

THE LONGHAIRS

The first longhairs seen in Europe are said to have been taken to Italy by the traveller, Pietro della Valla, (1586–1652) and at the end of the sixteenth century 'Ash coloured, Dun and speckled cats, beautiful to behold' with long coats were sent to France by the learned archaeologist, naturalist and scientist, Nicholas Claude Fabri de Peirese. It is believed that these early cats may have come from Angora (now Ankara) in Turkey. From France they spread to Britain, where for a time they were referred to as French cats, and then throughout the world.

Later travellers also brought cats from Persia which differed from the Angoras, whose heads were small, with longish noses, and tall ears, whereas the Persians had broader heads, smaller ears, shorter noses, and instead of the long silky coats of the Angoras had longer and thicker fur.

Early writers referred to both varieties. By the beginning of the nineteenth century, however, the Persian cats were preferred to the Angoras, but there was obviously cross-breeding, and soon the name Angora was dropped as their type disappeared. It is strange that even today there appear to be two types of coats in the longhairs, some long and silky, with less tendency to matt, and the others thicker and fuller, inclined to tangle.

It was in 1890 that Persians were much sought after by the Americans, and many cats were taken to the United States to found the Cat Fancy there. In Britain in 1901 the following colours and coat patterns were seen in their classes at the early shows: Black, White, Blue, Orange, Cream, Sable, Smoke, Tabby, Spotted, Chinchilla, Tortoiseshell, Bicolour and Tricolour. Today there are well over fifty longhair varieties recognised, with still more being produced by selective breeding. The name Persian was later dropped in favour of Longhair, although in North America they are still referred to as Persian.

For most Longhairs the standards require similar type and characteristics, apart from the coat colour and pattern. Each variety has a standard of 100 points, which is allocated to the characteristics required, i.e. the Black standard has 25 points for the coat colour, whereas the Blue has 20 points. A 'Standard of Points' is issued by the GCCF, and may be obtained from them. It is in loose leaf form, and as new varieties are recognised pages can be added. Briefly, the standard calls for the heads to be round and broad, with short broad noses, small tufted ears, large round eyes, with the colour according to the variety, cobby bodies on short thick legs, full dense coats, and short full tails. Kinks and undershot jaws are considered defects. Each variety is allocated a breed number, which is given in brackets after the different varieties in the following descriptions, but these may be changed in the near future as the GCCF have now installed a computer. (See also the Appendix.)

Black (1)

One of the earliest varieties which was very popular at the beginning of the century, when some fine cats were exhibited at the shows, and a number were exported to the United States. They are much liked there. In Britain, although there are some magnificent Blacks, they are not one of the most popular varieties, which is a great pity. It may be something to do with the

Black.

appearance of the kittens. They are born black, but the coats often take on a rusty look, and there may be white or grey hairs in the coat. It may be some months before the jet black fur is seen, contrasting well with the big round deep copper eyes.

Grooming is very important, and talcum powder should never be used as there may be some left in the fur, which will look like scurf. Breeders recommend using a little bay rum, sprinkling into the coats, brushing out, then polishing the coat with a chamois leather or piece of silk. If the cat is to be shown, it should be remembered that the coat turns brown in hot sun, and also in wet and damp, so if it is to look at best on the show day both should be avoided if possible.

Whites (2, 2a and 2b), *Plate 1*

Many of the original cats that came from the East were white, many with blue eyes. A few were said to be sulky and unresponsive, but it was later that they realised that there was an element of deafness which did affect some white cats with blue eyes. The early Angoras were chiefly white, and so were some of the cats from Persia. Cross-breeding followed, which resulted in some cats having blue eyes, others orange eyes, and some with one eye blue and one orange. At the early shows they were all entered in the same class, but because those with orange or copper eyes invariably had the preferred Persian type they always beat the others. Eventually they were divided into two classes, one for the blue-eyed and the other for the orange or copper, but the odd-eyed had to be shown as 'Any Other Variety', until the breeders protested that it was unfair, and the odd-eyed were also given their own class at the show.

Whites are one of the most popular of the longhairs, with really excellent ones being exhibited. The Best in Show is quite frequently an orange-eyed White, looking really beautiful. The type of the blue-eyed has improved over the years, and some also do well. The odd-eyed are comparatively few, but they are always an attraction at the shows.

The kittens are very pink when first born, but in a few weeks the fur grows and they take on the appearance of animated powder puffs.

Some people are worried about having a White and the problem of keeping them looking really sparkling white. Normally they can be kept looking beautiful by using talcum powder or baby powder sprinkled right into the roots and brushed right out. Many fanciers bath their Whites a few days before a show and when dry brush the coat thoroughly, making the fur around the head form a frame for the face. The tail too should receive special attention, being brushed out until it is nearly as wide as the body. If when showing a cat powder is left in the fur it may well warrant disqualification.

In North America the Whites are one of the Persian colours, with the standard calling for coats of pure glistening white, with the same type and characteristics for the three eye colour variations. All the Persians tend to be typier than in Britain, with shorter noses, and having judged them I found that the coats are more luxurious.

In North America they have the Turkish Angoras which may be all-white, although other colours are recognised, but the type is very much the same as the original Angoras, not like the Persian. The heads are small to medium, and wedge-shaped, with pointed ears set high on the head, and a longish nose. The body is small to medium on long legs, and the tail long and tapering. The coat is of medium length, fine and silky. The three eye colours are recognised in the Turkish Angoras. The coat colours too can be the same as for the Persians.

In Britain, there are Turkish cats, but they have auburn markings on the coat (see Turkish).

Blue (3), *Plate 2*

The Blues appeared at the first shows in the 'Any Other Variety' class, but in no way did they resemble the outstanding Blues we have today. They were really Blue Tabbies, or Blue cats with white markings. Frances Simpson showed the first pair of Blues in 1883 and they created a sensation as no one had seen any 'of this peculiar shade before'. By 1899 the Crystal Palace schedule had a class for Blue Self coloured, without white. In 1890 the class was divided into male and female, with 8 males and 8 females. They were becoming so popular that in the next year there were 15 males and 17 females. At Crufts Show in 1894, a blue male, Wooloomooloo, beat everything, and afterwards he won every time shown. He was responsible for breeding outstanding kittens, and many of today's winning Blues' pedigrees go back to him.

The problem with the early Blues, as well as getting rid of white patches, was the eye colour, which tended to be green. In 1903 those with green eyes had to be shown in the Any Other

Odd-eyed white.

Red Self.

Variety class. Cross-breeding with Blacks brought about a change, and most cats now have deep orange or copper eyes.

In 1901, the Blue Persian Cat Society was formed, the first longhaired breed club in the world, and when the GCCF came into being in 1910 they were granted the right to have two delegates in perpetuity. Visitors to the early shows took many of the Best Blues of that time back with them to the States, to carry off the highest honours there. They are one of the most popular varieties not only in Britain but also in North America.

The kittens are born with tabby markings, which disappear with age, with the fur growing rapidly. Any shade of blue is recognised, as long as it is the same colour right down to the roots. Talcum powder may be used on the coats to remove any dirt or dust, and the fur should be brushed up around the head to form a ruff.

The Blues bred nowadays come very close to

the set standard, and are used in the breeding of other varieties. Mated to a cream female, a blue male will sire blue-cream and cream males; and a blue female mated to a cream male may have blue-creams and blue males. A blue male mated to a blue-cream female may produce blue females, blue-cream females, blue males and cream males.

Red Self (4)

Reds were included in Harrison Weir's 'Points of Excellence' (the first Standards) but they were known as Oranges then, with the colour to be 'a brilliant sandy or yellowish colour'. Strangely enough Red is included in the colours for the early Angoras. By 1910 they were known as Red or Orange, with separate classes for the Red and Orange Tabbies. Later the classes were for Red Tabbies and Red Self or Shaded, and the colour 'Orange' was no longer used. Because of the various mixed breedings, most of the first reds were males, as no one realised that to produce red females it was necessary for both the male and the female to be pure-bred red. It used to be said that a red female was very valuable because they were so rare, but now with the correct breeding they are easy to produce.

As it is possible for both Selfs and Tabbies to appear in the same litter, it may be some weeks before it is possible to decide which the kittens are. The type is usually very good, with good broad head, short broad nose, small ears, and the beautiful large round deep copper eyes. Reds can be used in Cameo breeding, and mated to Tortoiseshells may produce self-coloured Creams, Blacks, Blue, and also Tortoiseshells.

Regular grooming is important with a few drops of bay rum sprinkled into the fur, and then brushed and combed, the coat being polished with a chamois leather.

Reds are included in the solid colours in North America, and the colour should be a deep

rich clear brilliant red. There are some magnificent specimens seen at the shows. There is also a variety known as Peke-faced, which may be solid or tabby Red. The Peke-faced has the shortest of noses, and the standard says that the head should resemble that of the Pekinese dog, with the nose very short, or indented between the eyes, with a decidedly wrinkled muzzle. The eyes are striking, being large round, full and brilliant copper. They are not recognised in Britain, as it is considered that they are over-typed, and could possibly have breathing problems, but in North America they are much admired, and frequently appear as Best in Show. It is possible for the Peke-faced to appear in normal Red Tabby or Self litters.

Cream (5)

The Creams had an unfortunate start in the Cat Fancy as they appeared frequently by chance in litters produced by the early Oranges (Red). Because of their dingy colouring they were

Creams.

referred to as Fawns, looked on as 'sports', and were given away as pets. Some were sent to the States, where they were liked. The early Creams often had a dark line along the spine and had barring or tabby markings on the heads, legs and tails. They were referred to as 'freaks or flukes' and were shown in the 'Any Other Variety' classes. The first classes they were given were for Creams and Fawns, with all shades of fawn allowed.

It was to be many years before enough was understood about breeding and it was found possible by selective breeding to produce cats that were really cream. By the 1920s they did begin to improve, with matings between Creams and Tortoiseshells producing quite good Creams. Really outstanding cats appeared from matings between Creams and Blues, and also another new variety, Blue-creams, which were females only. Over the years the type has steadily improved, and today most have the required longhaired type, with the big round deep copper eyes.

A Cream female mated to a Blue can have Cream males and Blue-cream females; and a Cream male mated to a Blue-cream may have both male and female Creams, Blue male kittens and Blue-cream kittens all in the same litter. They may also be used in matings with Tortoiseshells, Tortie and Whites, Blacks as well as Blues, and Bi-colours.

Faults are bars and tabby markings, and what is known as 'hot', meaning that the fur along the back may look a reddish colour; the stomach should not be white, nor the tip of the tail. Choosing the right mate is very important, so any faults are not increased. As with most longhaired Selfs, the kittens are born with tabby markings which go with growth. The colour should be pale to medium cream, pure and sound, with no shadings. Grooming is as for the Blues.

The Creams have always been very popular in North America, where the colour in the Standard is a level shade of buff cream, without markings. The lighter shades are preferred. The nose leather and paw pads are pink, and the large round eyes a brilliant copper, giving the face a sweet expression. The nose should be short, snub and broad, with a 'break'.

Smokes (6 and 6a), *Plate 3*

It is a pity that, as Black Smokes and Blue Smokes were among the varieties at the early shows in Britain, there are so few of them about now. They were produced by cross-breedings between Blacks, Whites and Blues. In 1893 they were given an open class, and it was said then that 'The Smoke is a cat of great beauty but unfortunately is rare.'

Known as the 'cat of contrasts', the undercoat should be white, with the tips shading to black, the body colour shading to silver on the sides, with a black mask on the face, and the frill and ear tufts should be silver. From a distance the coat appears to be black, and it is not until the cat walks that glimmers of the silver can be seen. There is also a Blue variety with 'blue' replacing 'black' in the standard.

The kittens are born black or blue, depending on the breeding, and it is very difficult, unless you are an experienced breeder, to determine for the first few weeks whether they are self-coloured or Smokes. Very close examination may show little white smudges of white around the eyes, and a lightish hue on the stomach. It can be many months before the really striking contrasts are clearly seen, in fact a Smoke may not look at his best until the adult coat is fully grown.

Grooming is very important for the Smokes, with the white undercoats being brushed up to gleam through the black top coats. The kittens may take on a rusty appearance before their true colouring is seen. As with the Blacks the coats are quickly affected by damp and strong sun. Smoke may be mated to Smoke, but this may result in some loss of type. A very good Black or Blue, depending on the top coat colour, could be used as a mate.

A comparatively recently recognised variety in Britain, but one which had championship status in North America some years ago, is the Cameo Red Smoke. These cats are very pretty, with red face masks, frill and ear tufts white,

Silver Tabby.

with the body red shading to white on the sides and flanks; the undercoats are as nearly white as possible. The eyes may be deep orange or copper. There are also Cream Smokes with cream tippings replacing the red. None of these varieties should show any form of tabby markings.

There is a female-only Smoke Tortoiseshell, with the tipping in the form of well-defined black, red and cream, broken into patches, with the colours to be bright and rich, and the face to have the same coloured patching. The undercoat should be pure white. This variety is recognised both in North America and Britain.

The type in all varieties should be typically longhair, with broad heads, small neat ears, snub noses, big round orange or copper eyes, and long dense and silky coats, and short bushy tails.

Tabbies

In Britain there are three colours of Tabbies recognised, but all should conform to the same classic tabby pattern. Harrison Weir considered that the tabby pattern was first introduced into the longhairs by matings with the English (British) Tabby. The pattern of markings requires that there should be an 'M' mark on the forehead, with delicate pencillings around the eyes. Looking down on the shoulders the markings take the shape of a large butterfly, made of small ovals and two fairly wide bars running down the back on each side of the spine. Around the chest should be two unbroken lines, like necklaces. The legs should be ringed, and also the tail, ending in a solid tip.

Silver Tabby (7)

At the early shows the Silver Tabby classes were well filled, but the photographs show that the markings were inclined to be solid, and the judges' reports said that the 'Silver tabby classes were full of nondescript cats'. Princess

63

Victoria of Schleswig-Holstein owned several that were said to be good. The Chinchillas are thought to have evolved from the Silvers, and they came to be preferred to the Tabbies, especially as it proved difficult, and still does, to breed them with the distinct markings showing up in the long fur. As the eyes have to be green or hazel so it is very difficult to find a longhair that can be used to improve the type.

The best Silver Tabbies are very dark when born, but do grow up into beautiful specimens. Faults are brindling in the coat, and yellowish marks. The standard now is for green or hazel eyes, but the early fanciers thought they should be hazel, as then Brown Tabbies or Blacks could be used to try to improve the type. Careful grooming is necessary to show the markings at their best.

Brown Tabby (8), *Plate 4*

One of the oldest varieties, with a number at the shows. At the Crystal Palace show in 1896 a Brown Tabby, Birkdale Ruffie, won everything, and also had a framed photograph, autographed by the Prince of Wales (later Edward VII), presented to him personally by the Prince. Frances Simpson's Persimmon (see p. 34) was an outstanding Brown Tabby for his day, judging by the early photographs. Another constant winner, King Humbert, was sent to the States in 1885 to Mr T. Barker, who refused an offer of 1,000 dollars for him made by a New York millionaire.

In Britain the colour should be rich tawny sable, but the American standard asks for brilliant coppery brown. The same markings of dense black are required for both. The American tabbies are more like the type than the Brpish.

The kittens are delightful and there is a ready demand for them, but they are usually bought as pets, and are neutered which does not help the breed very much.

Red Tabby (9)

(See also Red Selfs.) These were the early

Oranges and first appeared in classes with the Brown Tabbies. The pattern of markings can be clearly seen at birth, which may or not fade as the fur grows. The sex too will depend on the breeding, as a Tortoiseshell mated to a Red Tabby could result in red, tortie and black kittens, among others. Pure Red Tabby to pure Red Tabby can produce both red males and females. Faults are too long a nose, pale fur on the tummy and white hairs in the coat.

Blue Tabby

In North America very attractive Blue Tabbies have appeared in litters of Brown Tabbies. They are one of the rarer colours, with the ground colour a pale bluish ivory, with deep blue markings making a good contrast, giving an overall effect of a warm fawn overtone. They can be produced from Solid Blue and Brown Tabby matings. They were granted championship status in 1962. One or two have appeared in Britain, but they have no standard as yet.

It is also possible to have a Cream Tabby with very pale cream ground colour, and markings of buff or cream standing out from the background. Patched Tabbies too are being bred in the States. They may have a silver background, with dense black markings, and patches of red and/or cream; a brown background with similar markings; or a blue background again with similar markings. They are unknown in Britain.

All the colours may appear with a mackerel tabby pattern of markings, instead of the classic. This pattern is rarely seen in Britain in the longhairs. Mackerel markings are supposed to resemble those of the fish. The head markings are the same as the classic, but there should be a narrow unbroken line running from the back of the head to the base of the tail. The body should be covered with narrow lines which run vertically down from the spine lines. These lines to be narrow and numerous as possible.

Chinchilla (10), *Plate 5,* and Shaded Silver

The Chinchilla is one of the most striking

Blue Tabby.

varieties, and quite glamorous-looking with the pure white coats being delicately tipped with black, giving a sparkling effect, and making a beautiful contrast with the brilliant emerald or blue-green large round eyes, outlined with black or brown rims. The type should be as for the other longhairs. In Britain they tend to be lighter-boned, but are by no means delicate.

One of the first man-made varieties, they are thought to have evolved from lightly marked Silver Tabbies, and later possibly from Silvers mated to Whites. John Jennings writing in 1893 said 'The Chinchilla is a peculiar but beautiful variety; the fur at the roots is silver, and shades to a decided slate hue.' Mr C. House, a judge and writer on cats said a Mrs Vallance was the first to give the name Chinchilla to the variety. Her first Chinchilla was called Chinnie, and apparently was the result of chance mating of 'a maiden of high degree being wooed by a gay and gallant roamer who belonged to no one

knew whom, and had no known home.' He went on to say that Chinnie was really a light lavender, but when she was three years old she produced some beautiful kittens, with one of her daughters giving birth to a kitten that amazed the Cat Fancy. This was Silver Lambkin who became the first Chinchilla male. The first shown had golden eye colour, and when one owner had a Chinchilla with green eyes she was not allowed to show her.

Many of the early cats had light coats, but others were dark, and for a while there was confusion as to what a Chinchilla should really look like. At first there were two varieties, one with light tippings, and another with much heavier, and having a darker appearance, referred to as Shaded Silver, the eyes being green or orange. It became increasingly difficult to distinguish between the two, and when a cat at one show in 1902 received a prize as a Chinchilla and another as a Shaded Silver the Shaded Silver standard was withdrawn. It was still recognised in America, Australia, New Zealand

Shaded Silver.

and other countries, and is now being bred again in Britain, and should be re-recognised in the near future.

It is now much easier to distinguish between the two varieties, as the Shaded Silver standard says that the undercoat should be white with black tippings shading down from the sides, face and tail from dark on the ridge to white on the chin, chest, stomach, and under the tail, giving the appearance of a mantle. The eyes may be green or blue-green.

The Chinchillas and Shaded Silvers in the States are inclined to be of slightly heavier build, and the noses a little shorter.

When first born, the kittens are very dark, with bars and shadow rings on the tail, looking very unlike the 'fairy-like' cats seen at the show. Eventually the coat clears, and the white undercoat and tippings make their appearance.

In the States there are also Golden Chinchillas and Golden Shaded, with rich warm cream undercoat, tipped with seal brown, giving a golden effect. The tippings are heavier in the Shaded. They are being bred in Britain, but have not yet received championship status. There is a proposal that they should be known as Golden Persians.

Tortoiseshell (11), Tortoiseshell and White (12), *Plate 6*

A female-only variety, the Torties, as they are referred to, have very little background history, unlike most of the other longhairs. Occasional males are born, but do not sire kittens as a rule. There are the few claims that males have sired, but when seen they prove to have some faint bars or tabby marks on the coat, and are not true Torties.

In the National Cat Club stud book for 1900–1905, there are fifteen Torties entered, but few have a pedigree. Those that have seem to have come from Miss M. Beal's breeding, using her stud Romaldkirk Midshipmite, a Cream, mated to Wallflower, a Tortie. Others were bred by mating a Black, Johnnie Fawe, to Dainty Diana, a Tortie. Harrison Weir said he thought they had resulted in the beginning from short-

Golden Persians.

haired farm Torties mating with longhaired Blacks. With or without pedigrees they have always been much liked, and there is a ready sale for the kittens, as the pedigree ones are quite rare.

Over the years a number of different matings have been tried, using Blacks, Blues, Reds and Cream, but even today it is difficult to breed a Tortie to order. Tabbies cannot be used as they may introduce tabby markings which are very difficult to breed out.

The standard says that there should be three colours in the coat, black, red and cream, with the colours to be bright and rich. The distinctive patching should be well interspersed with the black, and there should be no brindling. A cream or red mark, known as a blaze, coming from the forehead to the nose, is much liked. The red should be a bright red, never ginger or sandy, and there should be tiny patches on the ears, and on the paws. The eyes should be deep orange or copper.

Torties make good mothers, and the resultant litters may be of mixed colouring, and even contain Torties. The kittens are very alert and lively, and most attractive to see.

The Tortie and White is also a female-only variety, with similar coloured patches as the Tortie, but with the addition of White. They used to be called Chintz cats in Britain and are still known as Calico in North America, as they are thought to resemble the materials.

They used to be just as difficult to breed as the Torties, but a British breeder who first produced Bi-colours, with coats of Red and White, Black and White, Cream and White, and Blue and White, used a selective breeding programme and found that, by mating Bi-colours bred from Tortie and White females to Tortie and White females, she could produce Tortie and Whites almost to order.

The colours are even more striking than those of the Tortie, with black, red and cream, or dilutions, to be well distributed patches, interspersed with white. The colours should be as bright as possible, and the white should not be overbearing. The type is as for all the longhairs, and is usually very good. The eyes may be deep

Dilute Tortoiseshell and White.

copper or orange in Britain and brilliant copper in North America. The coats do not seem to matt up as much as other longhairs, but a daily brushing and combing is still essential.

In North America the standard is for white with unbrindled patches of black and white. White should be predominant on the under-parts. There is also a dilute Calico, which is white with unbrindled patches of blue and cream. In Britain they are referred to as Dilutions or Tri-colours, and are judged in the same class as the Tortie and Whites.

Bi-coloured Longhairs (12a)

In the early days cats having two-coloured coats were known as Pieds or Magpies, as they were frequently black and white. Bi-colours have been bred in Britain for many years, but were considered to be of no use and sold as pets. As mentioned in the previous section, a breeder

Black and White Bi colour.

Blue and White Bi-colour.

realised that they could be very useful in breeding the elusive Tortie and Whites. The first standard recognised was based on the markings of the Dutch rabbit, which had very definite divisions of colour. In fact they were so precise that no breeder was able to produce cats with such markings, and eventually it was revised to read 'Not more than two-thirds of the coat to be colour and not more than half to be white. The face to be patched with colour and white.' Any solid colour with white is allowed.

In the States the standard says that they may be black and white, red and white, blue and white, cream and white, and also says that an inverted 'V' blaze on the face is desirable.

As mentioned before it is possible to breed Tortie and white by mating a Tortie and White to a Bi-colour male with a Tortie and White mother. A Bi-colour may be mated to another Bi-colour, but the type may not always be good, and an outcross may help to improve this.

However, some self-coloured kittens may be produced from such matings.

Bi-colour males are usually very large cats, strong and healthy. The silky full coat should have definite division of colour, and there should be no white hairs in the self colour. Grooming should be done so that the two colours appear at their best and are kept distinct from one another.

Blue-cream (13)

This is now a very popular sex-linked variety, but when kittens with blue and cream coats were born in litters at the end of the nineteenth century, after the fawns or creams had appeared, they were looked on as oddities. Various cross-breeding was tried in the early days, and sometimes the resultant kittens were thought to be of little importance, and given away. The standard today is for the blue and cream to be softly intermingled, but the first kittens had patched coats, and were frequently

Blue-cream.

referred to as blue tortoiseshells. Blue-creams are sometimes born in litters from tortoiseshells too. It became realised that, by mating a Blue-cream to a Blue or Cream male, not only was the coat colouring much improved but more often than not it contained the two colours intermingled, and also the type was very good.

They were recognised by the GCCF in 1929 after planned careful breeding was producing kittens with the two colours intermingled, giving a shot-silk or misty haze effect. Patches still appeared; even today a cat will have small patches somewhere, maybe on the face or a paw.

The standard says that the head should be broad and round with tiny ears, short broad nose, and intermingled fur on the face. The body should be short and cobby on short thick legs, the coat dense, soft and silky, and many Blue-creams answer nearly all these requirements.

Breeding Blue-creams can be very interesting as, being females only, with the choice of a Blue male or Cream as a mate, the sexes of the kittens can be varied. A Blue-cream mated to a Blue may produce Cream males, Blue males, Blue females and Blue-cream females; but mated to a Cream may produce Cream females, Cream males, Blue males and Blue-cream females.

The American standard for the Blue-cream differs from that of the British as it requires a blue coat with patches of solid cream, with the patching being clearly defined and well broken on both body and extremities.

Colourpoint (Himalayan) (13b 1–20), *Plate 7*

In 1947 Mr Stirling Webb, a well-known breeder of Siamese, was shown a cat that had been produced by chance and which intrigued him as it had longish fur, but with Siamese coat and points colouring. He thought this cat most attractive and there and then decided to start a breeding programme in the hope of producing cats with similar colouring, but having a longer coat, points colouring, and deep blue eyes. To produce a man-made breed is a long and expensive business, frequently meeting with disappointments on the way, with many kittens having to be neutered and given away as pets. By using the best Siamese and outstanding Blue and Black Persians, after eight years of planned breeding, Stirling Webb had succeeded and Colourpoints were granted recognition in 1955.

By a strange coincidence at almost the same time, a similar breeding programme was being carried out in North America. There the cats were called Himalayans, as they had similar colouring to the rabbits of the same name, but they were just like the Colourpoints in Britain.

Colourpoints bred by Stirling Webb and a fellow breeder, Mrs S. Harding, were exported to North America, and by the early 1960s they had been recognised by all the American Associations. The greatest difficulty in the past was to get the correct deep blue eyes and the typical longhair type. Over the years this has happened so well that some superb cats have been exhibited and are frequently Best in Show. They have good broad heads, short broad noses,

Litter of Blue, Cream and Blue-cream kittens.

Blue Colourpoint.

with distinct stops, the ears small and the cheeks full. Cobby cats on low legs, with short full tails, they must in no way resemble Siamese, except in their coat pattern.

The original Colourpoints were sealpointed with cream bodies, and seal-brown points, or blue, with glacial white body colourings, and blue points; the mask, ears, legs and tails should all be the same contrasting solid colour.

It took many years to produce the Seal and Blues, but it was soon realised that by selective breeding it was possible to produce Colourpoints with a great variety of points. At the moment there are twenty recognised variations such as Chocolate, Lilac Red, Tortie, Cream, Blue-cream, Chocolate Tortie, Lilac Cream, and various Tabbypoint colourings, including the original Seal and Blue, but not all are seen at the shows yet.

The kittens are born cream-coloured, with pink noses, ears and foot pads. The points colouring begins to appear in a few weeks, but it may be eighteen months before the long silky coat and points are really seen at their best.

Young Sealpoint Colourpoint.

Shorthaired Colourpoint kittens (left Tortiepoint, right Redpoint).

Self Chocolate (50b) and Self Lilac (50c)

In the early experimental stages of the breeding for Colourpoints, Stirling Webb realised that it was also possible to breed these two varieties (in the States they are known as Self Chocolate and Lilac). Unfortunately he died before this part of his plans could be completed. Over the years other breeders have been interested, but it was found to be very difficult to breed them with the good coat colours and deep orange or copper eyes, and also good longhair type. In the past few years progress has been made, and they are improving. They now have their own classes at the shows, but the numbers shown are very few.

The Chocolate should have a coat of medium to dark chocolate, even colour all over, and the Lilac fur a pinkish dove grey, sound to the roots, with cobby body on short legs, and short full tails.

Birman (13c), *Plate 8*

The Birmans should never be confused with the Colourpoints, although they have similar colour, that is a light body with contrasting points. A unique feature is the white gloved paws, which are known as gauntlets on the back legs and which should cover the paw and then go up the back of the legs, finishing in a point, whereas the front gloves should be pure white, finishing in a straight line across the paw. The shape of the gloves is most important and misshapen ones are penalised when being

Self Chocolate.

Self Lilac.

Sealpoint Birman showing good gloves and gauntlets.

judged. The heads are not quite so broad and round as the typical longhairs; the ears are medium in size; the noses medium length, with no stop; the full chins slightly tapered. The eyes are almost round, and deep blue in colour. The fur (in the Seal pale beige with a slightly golden hue) is long and silky, with a full ruff around the necks. The tail should be medium in length and bushy. The American standard is very similar but says that the noses should be roman in shape, with the nostrils set low. The colours are Sealpoint, Bluepoint, Chocolate and Lilac, and other colours are possible. As the coats do not matt very easily, they are much easier to groom, but even so daily grooming is advised to keep them looking immaculate.

As to their origins, the legend is that many, many years ago they were the guardians of the temples in Burma, so when the first Birmans were sent to France in 1919 they were known as the sacred cats of Burma. They were recognised in France in 1925, but unfortunately almost died out during World War 2, but one breeder had kept a pair and managed to start breeding once again.

In 1960 two Tibetan Temple kittens were sent to the States, and it was realised that their history and appearance was much the same as the Birmans, and they must have had a similar origin. Birmans were imported from France into Britain in 1964/5, and soon proved very popular, as they seem to be throughout Europe, North America and many other countries.

Turkish (13d)

The Turkish cats were first introduced into Britain in 1956 from the district around the Van lake in Turkey. They have the early Angora type, with short wedge-shaped heads, large ears, longish noses, pink-rimmed amber-coloured eyes, and longish bodies on medium length legs. The long, silky fur should be chalk white, with auburn markings on the face, with a

75

Turkish.

white blaze, and the tails should have faint auburn rings, and be of medium length. They have the reputation for swimming in warm pools and shallow streams. They were given championship status some years ago, but they are still comparatively rare here.

In America they are known as the Turkish Angoras, but they do not have the auburn markings. They are very like the first Angoras seen in Britain, but were imported into the States direct from Turkey. Some came from the zoo in Ankara where they are still being bred. The originals were white, with blue eyes, and odd eyes, but all colours are now recognised, including Black, Blue, Smokes, Tabbies, Calico and Bi-colour. The blue-eyed are sometimes affected by deafness, whereas the odd-eyed may be deaf on the blue side and have hearing on the other. Very alert and intelligent cats, they are being exported from the States to many other countries, as are the Turkey cats from Britain.

Cameos (51–2)

Cameos were first seen in America in 1954, having been produced by cross-breeding using Smokes and Torties, Silvers and Reds. Chinchilla crosses were also tried, but this meant the introduction of green eye colouring, which proved very difficult to breed out. The eyes should now be brilliant copper. The Smoke Cameos have already been mentioned in with the Smokes, but all the Cameos should have

Shaded Cameo.

pure white undercoats with tippings.

Comparatively recently in Britain, Australia, New Zealand and Europe, Cameos are beginning to appear in greater numbers. They have been produced by selective breeding and it is now possible to have Cameo Red Shell, Shaded, Tortie Cameo, and Red Smoke, also Cameo Cream Shell, Shaded, and Blue-cream Cameo.

All variations should have pure white undercoats, with the tippings being red or cream in the Shell and Shaded, black, red and cream in the Tortie, and blue and cream softly intermingled in the Blue-cream Cameo. The Smoke is as described in the Smoke section.

The Shell should have a sparkling silver appearance, with the coat being lightly dusted with pink or cream on the mask, along the spine, and on the legs and feet. Both the Shaded should have the white evenly shaded with red, giving the effect of a red mantle, or with cream giving the effect of a cream mantle. The Tortie's tippings should be black, red and cream, well broken into patches, and the Blue-cream with blue and cream tippings. It is also possible to have a Shaded Tortoiseshell. Tabby markings are faults. The eyes should be deep orange or copper. The type should be as for other longhairs, and because of the cross-breeding is frequently very good.

For the first two weeks it is very difficult to decide what the kittens will be, but as the fur grows and the contrasts appear, they become very attractive, and by the time the adult stage is reached most decorative.

Pewter (53)

This variety has a standard similar to that of the Shaded Silver, with a white undercoat shaded with black, giving a mantle-like effect. It was produced in the first place by mating Chinchillas and Blues, and later Blacks. The type is similar to other longhairs, with broad heads, neat ears, snub nose, firm chin with level bite. The eyes should be deep copper or orange.

The kittens are born very dark, with the coat lightening with age.

Maine Coon

These are mentioned elsewhere in the book as being one of the original cats with longish fur known in North America. Practically all colours are recognised there now, but the early ones were mostly tabby with white chests, which are still very much liked. These are massive cats, with medium-sized heads, large ears, and large eyes, with slightly oblique setting. The eyes may be any colour. The fur is thick and shaggy, being shorter on the shoulders and longer on the stomach and britches, with the tail being long and tapering, and very full.

They are not recognised in Britain, but one or two are now being bred here. In Europe, in Norway, there is a variety known as the Norwegian Forest Cat, which has a history similar to the Maine Coon, and has been known in Norway for hundreds of years. All coat patterns and colours are permitted, but most have some form of white on the chest and the paws.

THE SHORTHAIRS

The Shorthairs are divided into British, Foreign and Siamese. The British have very little history for the individual varieties, as over the years they have been produced by selective breeding with the original domestic cats, thought to have been introduced into this country by the Romans centuries ago. It has been possible to breed them in many different colours and coat patterns. Sometimes it took many years to get the exact characteristics required; for example, the Cream, which should be self-coloured all over, invariably had ringed tails.

After the first cat shows at the beginning of the century, the cats recognised were the Whites with blue eyes, Blacks, Blues, the Red, Silver and Brown Tabbies, and the female-only Tortoiseshell and the Tortoiseshell and Whites, also Pied, the two-coloured cats. In the early stud books many were from unknown parentage. The Manx are usually included in the British, although they are unique in that they are tailless. There are many stories as to their origin, a favourite being that there arrived on the Isle of Man a tailless cat that had swam ashore from a wrecked galleon from the defeated Spanish Armada, and she mated with a resident male and produced kittens like herself.

It is thought that in 1860 sailors from trading vessels sailing between Archangel and Britain sometimes brought back with them shorthaired cats with blue coats. These differed in looks from the resident Blues, which had typically British type, whereas those from Russia had slimmer bodies and short wedge-shaped heads, and green eyes. Both varieties were exhibited in the same class, and invariably the British cats won. This caused discontent among the exhibitors, so in 1912 the class was divided into Blue British type and Blue Foreign type. In 1939 the name Russian appeared in the stud book, although frequently they were referred to in early days as the Archangel cats. Unfortunately indiscriminate breeding between the two types meant loss of the original Russian type, and it almost disappeared. However a planned breeding programme was worked out, and today there are now Russians with very good type, and the typical short silky coats, with silver sheen, appearing at the shows.

The Abyssinian, another Foreign variety, is considered by many to be similar to the cats known long ago by the Egyptians, and certainly those they portray in their frescoes and statuettes are very like. In 1868 an Abyssinian known as Zula was brought to England when

Pewter.

the Military Expedition returned from service in Ethiopia (then Abyssinia). This cat had a ticked ruddy brown coat, and was thought to be very unusual. She must have been used for breeding, as in 1882 they were recognised as a separate breed. Both Harrison Weir and Louis Wain thought they should have been called Abyssinian type, as it was quite possible for such cats to appear in cross-matings between ordinary cats. This is true as I have seen them in South Africa among the street cats, and they really could be shown as Abyssinians. Anyway the name was dropped, and they were known as the British Ticks or Bunny, even Hare, cats, because of their coat colour. It was after the Abyssinian Cat Club was founded in 1919 that the name Abyssinian was used again.

The Burmese were first produced in the United States from a mating between a brown shorthaired female from Burma and a Siamese in 1930. The kittens were so liked that they soon became a recognised variety. They were imported in the late 1940s to Britain, two females, USA Champion Laos Cheli Wat, and Chindwin's Minou Twm, and a male, Casa Gatos da Foong. Other imports followed, and in a very short time they became extremely popular, and are bred in many different colours. They now rival the Siamese in numbers.

The first printed description of a cat with Siamese coat pattern was that recorded by Pallas, a noted explorer, in his book *Travels Through the Southern Provinces of the Russian Empire in the Years 1793–1794.* He wrote of a cat with the head longer towards the nose, with the body colour a light chestnut brown, with the ears, paws and tail quite black. The cat had three kittens exactly like herself.

It is frequently said that the first Siamese came to this country in 1884, but Siamese were shown at the Crystal Palace show from 1871 onwards, and Harrison Weir wrote that from 1871 to 1884 there were fifteen females and only four males at the shows. It is strange that the cat seen by Pallas had black points, as Siam means black, and I was told in Bangkok that was why the name was changed to Thailand. The Siamese were supposed to have come from the King's Palace and were jealously guarded, so at first they were known as the Royal Siamese.

BRITISH SHORTHAIRS

The pedigree British-type shorthaired cats are the selfs (White, Black, Blue and Cream) and the non-selfs (the Tabbies, Tortoiseshells, Tortoiseshell and White, Blue-creams, Bi-colours and Smokes). All these shorthaired cats are judged on the same standard of points, with minor variations according to coat colour and eye colour. The British Cat is compact, well balanced and powerful showing good depth of body, a full broad chest, short strong legs, rounded paws, tail thick at the base with a rounded tip. The head is round with good width between the ears, round cheeks, firm chin, small ears, large round and well-opened eyes with a short straight nose. The coat is short and dense.

Whites (14, 14a and 14b)

The Blue-eyed White should have a pure white coat, untinged with yellow and deep sapphire blue eyes, with no flecks or green rims. The Orange-eyed White should have gold, orange or copper eyes with no flecks or green rims, and the Odd-eyed White should have one blue eye and one eye gold, orange or copper with no flecks or green rims.

Black (15)

The Black should have a coat black to the roots with no rusty tinge and no white hairs any-where. Eyes should be deep copper or orange with no trace of green.

Blue (16), *Plate 9*

The Blue should have a coat of light to medium blue, even colour with no tabby markings or white anywhere, and no silver tipping. Eyes should be copper or orange with no green rims.

Cream (17)

The lighter shades are preferred in the coat colour of the Cream, and should be level in colour and free from markings with no sign of white anywhere. Eye colour should be copper or orange, and no green rims.

Tabbies

The Tabbies may be Brown, Red or Silver, classic or blotched pattern, mackerel or spotted. In the classic tabby pattern all markings should be clearly defined and dense. The legs should be barred evenly with bracelets going down from the body markings to the toes. Ground colour and markings should be equally balanced. The tail should be evenly ringed. On the neck and upper chest there should be unbroken necklaces, the more the better. On the forehead there should be a letter 'M' made by frown marks. There should be an unbroken line running back from the outer corner of the eye. There should be pencillings on the cheeks and a vertical line which runs over the back of the head and extending to the shoulder markings, which should be shaped like a butterfly. Both the upper and lower wings should be defined

Orange-eyed White.

Plate 1 Orange-eyed White Longhair

Plate 3 Black Smoke Longhair

Plate 5 Chinchilla

Opposite: Plate 4 Brown Tabby Longhair

Plate 6 Tortoiseshell and White Longhair

Plate 7 Sealpoint Colourpoint

Plate 8 Sealpoint Birman

Plate 9 British Blue Shorthair

Plate 10 British Red Classic Tabby Shorthair

Opposite: Plate 11 British Cream Tipped Shorthair

Plate 13 Abyssinian (Usual)

Opposite: Plate 12 Russian Blue

Plate 15 Dilute Tortoiseshell and White Cornish Rex

Opposite: Plate 14 Brown Burmese

Plate 16 Sealpoint Siamese

clearly in outline with dots inside this outline. On the back there should be a line running down the spine from the butterfly to the tail and there should be a stripe on each side of this running parallel to it. These stripes should be separated from each other by stripes of the ground colour. On each flank there should be a large solid oyster or blotch which should be surrounded by one or more unbroken rings. The markings on each side should be identical. All Tabby cats should be spotted in the abdominal region and should have evenly ringed tails.

In the mackerel tabby pattern the head, legs and tail are as for the classic tabby. There should be a narrow unbroken line running from the back of the head to the base of the tail. The rest of the body should be covered with narrow lines running vertically down from the spine line and unbroken. These lines should be as narrow and as numerous as possible.

Brown Classic Tabby.

Silver Tabby (18)

The Silver Tabby should have a clear silver ground colour with dense black markings. The eye colour may be green or hazel.

Red Tabby (19), *Plate 10*

The Red Tabby has a red ground colour and markings of deep rich red, the eye colour is a brilliant copper.

Brown Tabby (20)

The Brown Tabby has a brilliant coppery brown ground with dense black markings. The eye colour may be orange, hazel or deep yellow.

Spotted Tabby (30)

The Spotted Tabby has the mackerel stripes broken up to form spots which may be of any size or shape, round, triangular, rosette, lozenge or star shaped, but they must be clearly defined. It should have good clear spots in the appro-

Spotted Tabby.

priate colours, i.e. silver with black spots, brown with black spots, red with deep rich red spots, and eyes as with the appropriate colour variety. Occasionally cream and blue 'spotties' are bred.

Tortoiseshell (21), Tortoiseshell and White (22)

The Tortoiseshell (female only) is a black cat with brilliant patches of cream and red which should be clearly defined and well broken. A red or cream blaze on the head is desirable. Eyes should be brilliant copper or orange. The Tortoiseshell and White Shorthair (female only) has black, cream and red on white equally balanced. The tri-colour patchings should cover the top of the head, ears and cheeks, back, tail and part of the flanks. A white blaze is desirable. Eye colour should be copper or orange.

Dilute Tortoiseshell and White.

Tortoiseshell.

Manx (25, 25a and 25b)

The tailless Manx is an interesting breed, which does not 'breed true' – that is, Manx-to-Manx matings do not result in kittens. It is necessary for the partner of a tailless Manx to carry a gene for a normal tail in order to produce any progeny. The Manx gene can cause malformations in other parts of the body as well as the tail, such as Spina bifida, and stillbirths and early deaths are common in the litters born. So Manx kittens are scarce and show a great variability. For exhibition purposes, the Manx is divided into four groups: Rumpies, the true exhibition Manx, which are completely tailless, sometimes having a 'dimple' at the base of the spine; Rumpy-risers, which have a small 'knob' made up of a small number of tail vertebrae; Stumpies, or Stubbies, the Manx with a definite tail stump; and Tailed or Longies with a shortened, almost normal tail. The Manx cat has a characteristic bobbing, rabbit-like gait, the 'Manx hop' and a distinct double coat.

The Governing Council of the Cat Fancy recognises the Manx cat in any colour or pattern. The overall impression of a Manx cat is that of 'roundness'.

Blue-cream (28)

The Blue-Cream (female only) has a blue and cream, softly intermingled coat and no blaze. There should be no tabby markings or white anywhere. Eye colour may be copper or orange.

Bi-coloured Shorthairs (31)

The Bi-colour comes in any accepted self colour and white. The patches of colour should be clear and evenly distributed. Not more than two thirds of the coat should be coloured and not more than one half white. The face should be patched with colour and preferably there should be symmetry in the distribution of colour. A white blaze is desirable. Eye colour should be brilliant copper or orange.

Smoke.

Smoke (36)

Smokes may be black or blue with a pale silver undercoat and yellow or orange eye colour.

British Tipped Shorthair (39), *Plate 11*

A new variety recently granted official recognition is the British Tipped Shorthair. It is a shorthaired chinchilla; the majority of the coat is pale silver, the hairs having black tipping. There are blue, chocolate, lilac, red and cream versions also recognised.

FOREIGN SHORTHAIRS

Russian Blue (16a), *Plate 12*

The Russian Blue on the show bench today

Opposite above: Manx.   *Opposite below:* Blue-cream.

should be medium blue with no shading or tabby markings. The double coat is the most distinctive feature and very different from any other breed; it is short, thick and very fine, upstanding and silky like the coat of a seal. The silver tipping of the guard hairs reflects light, giving a silver sheen. The head is a short wedge with a flat skull, prominent whisker pads, and a strong chin. The body should be long and graceful in outline with long legs and small oval feet. The ears should be large and pointed, set upright. The skin of the ears is very thin, almost transparent; the eyes are vivid green, set wide apart and almond in shape. Russian Blues are affectionate cats, quiet-voiced and extremely hardy.

Abyssinian (23, 23a and 23c), *Plate 13*

The Abyssinian and its longhaired version, the Somali, are unique in the pedigree cat world. They have a unique ticked coat in which each hair has two or more dark bands together with residual tabby markings found on the head and

85

Sorrel Abyssinian.

sometimes on the tail and legs. Their body shape is a long, lean and powerful 'foreign type', but not as extreme as the Siamese. The head shape is moderately foreign, the ears are large and pointed, often with tufts, and pricked. The eye colour should be amber, hazel or green. The voice is quiet. The standard colouring is called 'Usual' or 'Normal', a rich golden brown ticked with black, preferably three bands of ticking. The base hair should be ruddy orange or rich apricot, the tip of the tail and the solid colour on the hind legs should be black.

The Sorrel Abyssinian should have a body colour of lustrous copper ticked with chocolate and the base hair deep apricot. The tip of the tail and the solid colour on the hind legs to be chocolate. The Blue Abyssinian should have a body colour of blue-grey with a soft warm

Russian Blue queen and kittens.

Blue Abyssinian.

87

Somali.

effect, ticked with deeper steel blue and the base hair oatmeal. The tip of the tail and the solid colour on the hind legs should be steel blue. All these three varieties have full Championship status.

As with many other breeds, new colours have been introduced and breeders are working towards recognition of the Chocolate, Lilac, sex-linked Red and Cream, together with six Tortie varieties. There is also a Silver Abyssinian, giving a further six varieties. Most of these are only at the Preliminary Standard stage or even only 'suggested Preliminary Standard' stage.

Somali

A recent arrival on the show bench is the Somali, a semi-longhaired Abyssinian. It should look exactly like an Abyssinian except for its coat which is long enough to show many bands of ticking and is silkier, softer and much longer.

It has a full tail like a fox's brush and is somewhat wild-looking, yet it has a gentle nature and is soft-voiced and friendly. As with the Balinese, the long-haired version of the Siamese cat, the Somali has been the subject of much controversy but it is now generally accepted that the longhair gene is carried in some lines of both these two breeds and that the appearance of longhair is not a mutation. Somalis have championship status in America and have been exhibited in Australia and New Zealand. They are also being bred in Europe.

Burmese (27, 27a–j), *Plate 14*

The Burmese is an elegant cat of foreign type which is positive and quite individual to the breed. There should be no suggestion of Siamese type or British cobbiness. The body should be of medium size, hard and muscular, legs should be slender with neat oval paws. The tail should be straight, of medium length tapering only slightly to a rounded tip. A visible kink or other bone defect is a fault. The head should be slightly rounded on top tapering to a short, blunt wedge. There should be no muzzle pinch. Ears should be medium in size with slightly rounded tips. There should be a distinct nose break and a strong chin. The eyes should be large and lustrous, set well apart, neither round, nor oriental, and any shade of yellow with golden yellow preferred. The coat should be short, fine and glossy, lying close to the body.

The official standard gives the various coat colours 'in maturity'. In all colours the underparts will be slightly lighter than the back. Kittens and adolescents may show faint tabby barrings and are a lighter colour than adults. The colour of the Brown Burmese should be a rich warm seal-brown with slightly darker ears and mask. The Blue Burmese should be a soft silver grey with a distinct silver sheen on ears, face and feet. In the Chocolate Burmese, the overall colour should be a warm milk chocolate; ears and mask may be slightly darker but evenness of colour is desirable. Lilac Burmese should have a coat of pale, delicate dove-grey

with a slightly pinkish cast. For the Red Burmese, the coat colour should be light tangerine with ears distinctly darker than the back, and slight tabby markings may be found on the face. The coat of the Brown Tortie Burmese should be a mixture of brown and red without obvious barring. The Cream Burmese should have a rich cream coat colour with ears only slightly darker than the back colour; as with the Red Burmese, slight tabby markings may be seen on the face. The Blue-cream Burmese (female only) coat should be a mixture of blue and cream without barring. The Chocolate Tortie Burmese coat should be a mixture of Chocolate and Red, without barring, and the coat of the Lilac Cream Burmese should be a mixture of lilac and cream.

In the case of the four tortie colours the coat may display two shades of its basic colours and may thus appear to show three or even four colours. The colours may be mingled or blotched; blazes, solid legs or tails are permissible.

The Burmese cat in all its colours is a

Chocolate Burmese.

Lilac Burmese.   Brown Tortie Burmese.

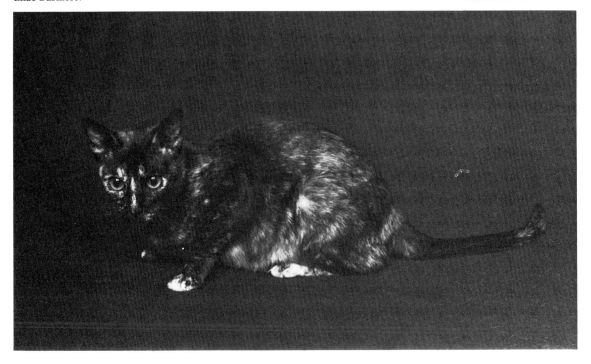

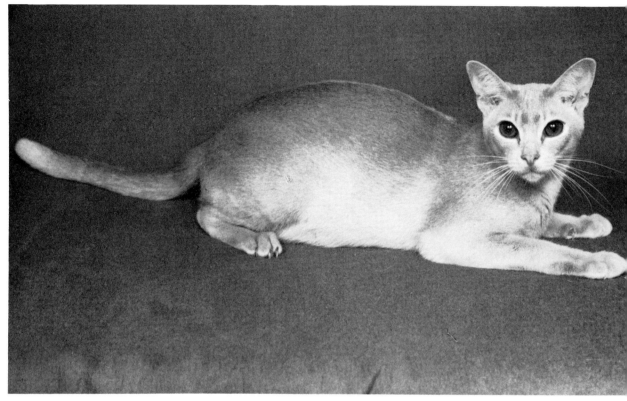

Cream Burmese.

beautiful animal, athletic, adventurous, full of curiosity and quite irrepressible, but loving and full of charm. They are wonderful companions and become very much attached to their owners.

Havana (29)

The Havana is a man-made breed derived from a cross between a self-coloured cat and a pointed Siamese. There were self-brown cats among the early imported Siamese in the 1880s but no attempt was made to establish an 'all-brown' breed until the 1950s, when a breeder crossed a self-black with a Siamese and another breeder crossed a Russian Blue with a Siamese. The first all-brown kitten was exhibited in 1953, but official recognition was not granted until 1958 when the name Chestnut Brown Foreign was given. In 1971 the name was changed to Havana which was the name the original breeders had wanted.

Many of the Havanas on the show bench in Britain today stem from an all-brown cat that was produced in a breeding programme to create the Foreign White. This brown cat, sired by a Lilacpoint Siamese, had its sire's body type and the potential to produce both brown and lilac kittens.

The coat colour should be a warm reddish-brown, short, glossy, even and sound throughout. Any tendency to black is penalised. The head should be long and well-proportioned, narrowing to a fine muzzle. The ears are large, wide at the base with good width between. The eyes are green, the body should be long and lithe, legs slim and paws oval. The tail is long and whip-like with no kink. Nose leather matches the coat colour, but paw pads should be pink.

The Havana is very intelligent, full of character with a charming nature. His voice is quiet and he is a happy, healthy and playful cat, a wonderful companion and a joy to watch.

Havana.

Foreign Lilac (29c)

A near relation of the Havana is the Foreign Lilac. Self Lilacs were first produced by the Laurentide line in the 1950s, harking back to the Russian Blue outcrossing, but as I remember them they were paler and pinker in coat colour, and not so 'Siamese' in type. They were granted the variety number 29c in 1974 to correlate with the Lilacpoint Siamese (24c). They are judged to the same standard as the Havana except for coat colour which should be a frosty grey with a distinct pinkish tone. The Foreign Lilac, with sparkling green eyes, is a most attractive addition to the show bench, equable in temperament, full of character, loving and lovable.

Cornish Rex (33) and Devon Rex (33a), *Plate 15*

These are the curly-coated cats and are relatively new on the show bench. Two distinct mutations turned up, the first in Cornwall in 1950 and the second in Devon, ten years later. Interbreeding resulted in straight-haired kittens, so they were officially recognised as two distinct breeds, and have been developed along different lines, giving a characteristic though different appearance to the two breeds.

The coat of the Cornish Rex is generally very dense and covers the cat in deep waves and curls; the Devon Rex cat is somewhat harsher and sometimes sparse, with bald patches. The Rex coat is devoid of guard and awn hairs, and about half the length of the normal coat; it is also thinner.

The Cornish Rex on the show bench should have a short, plushy coat, without guard hairs, which curls, waves or ripples, particularly on the back and tail. Whiskers and eyebrows should be of good length and crinkled. All coat colours are acceptable, but any white markings must be symmetrical (except in the female-only Tortoiseshell and White). The head should be a medium wedge with a strong chin. The skull is

Foreign Lilac.

flat and the profile straight from the centre of the forehead to the end of the nose. The cat should have oval eyes, not too large and in keeping with the coat colour. Ears should be large, set high on the head, with rounded tips and well covered with fine fur. The body should be slender and of medium length with long legs and small, oval paws. The tail should be long and tapering and well covered with curly fur.

The Devon Rex has a very short fine coat, wavy and soft without guard hairs. Whiskers and eyebrows should be crinkled, of medium length and rather coarse. All coat colours except bi-colours are acceptable, but without white markings other than in Tortoiseshell and White. The pixie-like head of the Devon Rex is quite unmistakable. The show standard calls for a wedge-shaped head with face full-cheeked, a short muzzle with a strong chin and a whisker

Cornish Rex.

break. The nose should have a strongly marked stop, and the forehead should curve back to a flat skull. The eyes should be set wide, large, oval and sloping towards the outer edges of the ears. Eye colour should be in keeping with the coat colour. The ears should be large, set rather low, very wide at the base, tapering to rounded tops, and well covered with fine fur. The body should be hard and muscular, slender and of medium length, with a broad chest and a slender neck. Legs should be long and slim, the hind legs longer than the fore-legs, with small, oval paws. The tail is long, fine and tapering,

well covered with fine fur.

The Rex cat is a very unusual, interesting animal, an affectionate, intelligent pet.

Korat (34)

A recent addition to the show bench is another blue cat, the Korat. It is a native of Thailand where it is called the Si-Sawat, and is relatively rare. The present-day Korat was established in the USA from carefully controlled breeding programmes to keep the breed pure. The head should be heart-shaped, and the muzzle neither pointed nor square. The ears are large with a rounded tip and set high on the head. The eyes

Devon Rex.

Korat.

are large and alert-looking, brilliant green in colour. A short nose and a strong chin, a muscular body, medium in size and semi-cobby. The tail is medium length with a rounded tip. The coat is single, short to medium in length, fine and glossy, lying close to the body; it is silver-blue all over, tipped with silver, without shading or tabby markings. Korats make intelligent and loving pets with quiet voices.

Foreign White (35)

Another relative is the Foreign White. A manu-factured breed built up from a 'coloured cat wearing a white overcoat' by very careful matings with first-class Siamese for several generations. It began in 1962. Carefully-formulated breeding programmes were fol-lowed and careful records were kept and only the very best offspring were used for breeding.

Breeding stock is carefully graded and some categories are not yet approved for white to white matings. The Foreign White has achieved a high degree of perfection. Full recognition, with Championship status, was granted in 1977 and the breed gained its first Grand Champion-ship in 1979.

The body should be lightly built, long and lissom with long legs and oval paws. The head should be long and wedge-shaped in profile, and the face should narrow in straight lines to a fine muzzle with a strong chin. The ears should be large, and pricked, with good width bet-ween. Eyes should be almond-shaped and slant-ing, and clear brilliant blue. The tail is long, tapering, whip-like with no kink. They are very intelligent, amiable and well aware of their beauty and elegance.

Foreign Black (37) and Foreign Blue (37a)

Over the years, other self colours have ap-peared. The Foreign Black was given provi-sional status in 1978 and has now progressed to Championship status and has achieved its first Grand Champion. The Foreign Blue was granted its breed number in 1981 and is now aspiring to full Championship status in 1984. Reds, Creams, and Tortoiseshells are standing on the side lines, together with the new colours Cinnamon and Caramel.

Oriental Spotted Tabby (38)

The Oriental Spotted Tabby is the first of the Siamese-type Tabbies to have full Champion-ship status. It was given breed recognition in 1978, and is seen in all the recognised colours, brown, blue, chocolate, lilac, red, cream and silver. Classic, mackerel and ticked (Abyssinian-type) tabbies are, as yet, only seen in Assessment Classes at shows. With the introduction of silver to the Siamese lines, a whole new range of coat colours has resulted.

Opposite: Foreign White.

Foreign Black.

Right: Foreign Blue.

Siamese (24, 24a–c, 32, 32a–c), *Plate 16*

The Siamese cat is one of the most popular breeds on the show bench. The striking appearance of the Sealpoint with its cream body and dark brown 'points' (mask, ears, legs and tail), and brilliant blue, oriental eyes, has always been a 'show stopper'. The Sealpoints, sometimes called Royal Siamese, were the first variety to be given breed recognition but over the hundred years since these cats were introduced to the western world many more coloured points have been officially recognised and have championship status. The Bluepoints were, for many years, regarded as freaks or sports, but 'very lovely animals with the palest of cream coats and lavender blue points. Sometimes the points are of a stone grey colour,

Above: Oriental Classic Tabby kitten.

Below: Oriental Ticked Tabby.

Oriental Spotted Tabby.

which detracts from their beauty.' One wonders if the 'lavender blue points' could have been today's Lilacpoints which must have been around, though not acknowledged, long before the Laurentide hybrids. The Chocolatepoint Siamese also appeared in litters long before they were officially known but had been treated as 'poor seals' and registered as Sealpoints. The points of this variety should be milk chocolate colour, but the tendency today is for the points to be much too dark though the body colour remains clear and cream. The true milk chocolate colour is now somewhat of a rarity and the difference in the colouring is sometimes referred to as the 'light phase' or 'the dark phase'.

The Lilacpoint Siamese was the last of the points colours to be granted a 24 breed number.

Most of today's lines stem from the outcross to a Russian Blue though there have been some non-hybrids, arising naturally.

Over the years other pointed Siamese had been seen but not acknowledged. The establishment of the Tabbypoints, Redpoints and Tortiepoints, all manufactured varieties, was the culmination of many years of dedicated perseverance by a few breeders, who had to combat the diehards for 'purity'. In 1966 they were granted the overall number of 32 with extensions, and today we have Tabbypoints and Tortie/Tabbypoints in all colours, Redpoints, Tortiepoints in the four basic colours and Creampoints. There are other colours but not yet approved.

The standard by which Siamese cats are judged is based on that for the Sealpoint, with specific amendments for the varying colours and patterns. The Siamese cat should be

Chocolatepoint Siamese.

Lilacpoint Siamese.

medium in size with a long, svelte body, long, slim legs, hind legs slightly higher than the front ones, feet small and oval, tail long and tapering and free from any kink. The head should be wedge-shaped, neither round nor pointed. It should be long and well-proportioned carried upon an elegant neck,

Seal Tortiepoint Siamese.

Above: Redpoint Siamese.

with width between the eyes, narrowing in perfectly straight lines to a fine muzzle, with straight profile, strong chin and level bite. Ears rather large and pricked, wide at base. The eyes should be blue, oriental in shape and slanting towards the nose. The points, that is the mask, ears, legs, feet and tail, should be a dense and clearly defined colour, matching in basic colour on all points, showing a clear contrast between points and body colour.

The Siamese cat is highly intelligent and easily trained. It is very demanding of love and attention and is not happy left alone. It makes a wonderful companion, demanding to be petted and played with, expecting you to understand what it says and giving you, in return, deep devotion.

Balinese (61, 61a–j)

The Balinese, the 'long-haired Siamese' is a Siamese cat that possesses two genes for long-hair and should be like a Siamese in every way except for a long coat and a plumed tail. The coat, although longer than the ideal Siamese coat, lies more or less flat along the body and there is no woolly undercoat. In all other respects it should resemble the Siamese and is judged to the same standards. In North America the Balinese bred in the four solid colours of Siamese, that is seal, blue, chocolate and lilac, have championship status, but longhaired Siamese in colours that are registered under the variety number 32 in Britain are known as Javanese. In temperament it is like the Siamese, agile, lively, affectionate, intelligent and beautiful.

Bluepoint Balinese.

6 Characteristics of the Cat

Anyone who lives with a cat, or cats, knows that each cat is different from the others. In a litter of kittens each has its own individuality — one will rush to meet you, another will run and hide, some will stand their ground and contemplate you, weighing you up, others will just get on with whatever they were thinking of doing when you approached them. Each cat or kitten has its own personality, but there are common characteristics and qualities.

The cat has never been completely tamed or understood. He is a solitary animal, very able to look after himself; he can survive all kinds of calamities. 'The cat has nine lives'; he goes his own way, does what he pleases, choosing his own time. It is easier to teach a cat not to do things than to do them. He will understand 'NO' and stop scratching the furniture so long as you are watching him, but that clever little trick you have taught him, to turn a somersault or jump through a hoop, certainly will not be performed to order. A cat is only obedient when he chooses to be. For his own convenience he has learnt to open doors, or to open refrigerators, and for his own amusement he will retrieve, but he will not fetch and carry with consistent reliability like a dog. A young kitten is 'trained' to use a sanitary tray; or is it instinct that prompts it to 'cover up'

British Cream with an outstanding litter.

'Chamber Music' by Henriette Ronner.

lest any marauder track it down? No cat has ever been trained to do a task.

Cats are not inherently social; they do not form groups or work as a team, but they are not entirely self-sufficient. Several house cats will live together, once a hierarchy has been established. Often there is keen rivalry until the 'boss cat' has been decided, and there can be animosity between varieties. Often though a pair of cats will form a devoted friendship, especially if there is no other cat to make a threesome.

Some cats will form a lasting friendship with a human being, but often only on their own terms; most cat-lovers can claim this devotion from one particular cat, but by and large the cat is pleasing itself. Margaret Cooper Gay, in *How to Live with a Cat*, says that 'we can all be sure our cats live with us because they love us, otherwise they'd leave', and 'they live with me because they like my company, and they pay board by keeping my house free of rodents, my

garden free of snakes and my heart young.' Perhaps keeping the house free of rodents is the reason that the cat has been kept by man over the centuries. He guarded the grain crops in ancient Egypt and has been guarding them ever since; farmers, millers, brewers, businessmen and government officials have all recognised the cat's usefulness as an efficient rat and mouse catcher. Unfortunately now the cat is being superseded by official rodent exterminators, and the use of pesticides. There used to be, however, official cats in the Home Office and the British Museum, and Whitehall had a series of black cats all named Peter (who was succeeded by a black female Manx named Peta).

Today, with the possibility of bringing rabies to Britain, there are fewer cats allowed on ships, and the Royal Navy has banned cats from warships. So now perhaps the cat is becoming less useful to man and more of a companion and a hobby.

Cats are intelligent creatures. Whether intelligence is acquired or whether it is inborn has always been debated, but it is certainly one of

'A School of Science and Art' by Henriette Ronner.

Hide and seek! A roll of carpet makes a good hiding-place.

This Brown Burmese has learnt to open the door, and is now teaching his playmates!

Two Red Tabby half-Persians at play.

the attributes of the cat. It is amazing how very young kittens, almost as soon as they leave the nest and start moving about, at around three weeks old, gather at a door knowing it will be opened; very soon they are scratching at the door to try to open it, and as they grow stretch to reach the door knob and rattle it. Many cats are able to open doors and windows, knowing full well that it is the knob or latch which operates the opening or closing. There are some cats that are brighter than others; all kinds of experiments, usually using food as an incentive, have been attempted to try and measure a cat's intelligence.

Cats recognise other cats. Even a kitten, seeing itself in a mirror, will investigate behind the mirror to find the kitten he saw. For the most part, they recognise each other by smell rather than by sight. When my cats gather together for a communal meal, there is always a sniffing session, first the head in welcome and then the tail region. One queen in particular inclines her head and always expects her daughter to 'kiss' her on her forehead. The newborn kitten finds its own teat by smell, and the male cat knows that the female is ready to accept him by smell. They also mark their own territory by rubbing. They have scent glands along the tail, on the forehead and on the lips and chin and in rubbing their heads on a chair leg or weaving round and round your feet, they are leaving their own mark of possession. There is another, less pleasant, way of marking their territory: spraying urine, which is one reason that only humans that have lost their own sense of smell tolerate an uncastrated tom in the house.

Another way cats mark their presence is by scratching or 'stropping' on certain trees, a particular door jamb, a gate post or a favourite chair.

Cats like routine and an ordered existence. They have a very good sense of time and will be ready and waiting 'on time' for their meals. There is a pattern to their day; they go out and take the same route, smell their previous 'markings', go to the same places, inspect yesterday's hunting ground and perhaps remain there for some time before returning, again by a fixed route. Cats also have remarkable homing abilities, and there are many instances of cats going back to their old homes after removals, sometimes turning up after a long period of time. Still more remarkable are the few cats that have been capable of finding absent owners in distant places where the cat has never been. In the USA there are 22 accounts of cats that are reputed to have done just that.

Cats have been thought to be able to predict rain, earthquakes and other disasters. There are stories of the household cat being the first in the air-raid shelter when a raid was imminent in World War 2. There are also many superstitions to do with cats; for example, to see a black cat on her wedding day is supposed to be a good omen for the bride. There is an old saying: 'Kiss the Black Cat and 'twill make ye fat, kiss the White one 'twill make ye lean.' Some people say that kittens born in May are dirty, and many people believe that a cat will not enter or remain in a house with a corpse. A cure for warts is to pass the tail of a black cat nine times over the warts. Some say that a stye on the eye can be cured by the same method.

The only certainty about the behaviour of cats is that each one displays an individual personality which is invariably captivating to its owner!

Right above: A Sealpoint Siamese begging.

Right: The same cat catching a ball of wool.

7 Modern-day Showing

When buying a pedigree kitten it as well to ask the breeder about its potentialities, even if not thinking then about breeding or showing. If it is being sold as a pet, the breeder may not want it exhibited; on the other hand if it is a really good kitten he or she would probably like it exhibited. Obviously the price paid for a really good show specimen will be very much more than for a pet. A kitten with an obvious fault, for example a Siamese with a white toe, could not be shown, but would still make a delightful pet. For more details of how to choose a good kitten for showing, see Chapter 8.

Having been advised by the breeder to do so, the new owner may think about showing, but find the whole idea rather frightening, but also exciting. However, there are several musts that are vital to the showing of a kitten. It must have been registered by the breeder, and the owner must have sent off the transfer form, with the correct money, at least three weeks before the show date. The kitten must have been inoculated against feline infectious enteritis, if this has not already been done, and the owner must have a current certificate issued by the veterinary surgeon, which should be taken to the show, as it may be asked for.

The kitten should be in first-class condition, with no signs of fleas in the coat, runny eyes, or dirty ears, and must be used to being handled, and not try to bite and scratch when picked up by strangers, as the judge and steward will be.

GREAT BRITAIN

Next will be the choice of shows, and one that is not too far away for the first time. It is not always easy to find out about the dates and location of shows, but the GCCF publish an annual list of shows for the coming year. It costs £1 from the GCCF (3–4 Penel Orlieu, Bridgwater, Somerset).

There are breed shows run by clubs for a specific variety or varieties, and the larger all-breed shows, organised by clubs interested in all varieties. There are also three types of show.

1) An Exemption Show, where the rules are not so strict as for other shows, where there are not so many classes or exhibits, and the judges may have time, once the judging has finished, to talk to exhibitors.

2) A Sanction Show, which is really a rehearsal for a Championship Show, with the same rules, but no challenge certificates are given.

3) A Championship Show, the most important, where challenge certificates are given, where the competition is fiercer, and where open class wins are very important to breeders. (There is also a Supreme Show, which will be described later.)

For a beginner an Exemption is the best

A judge summing up in her notes.

The array of prizes at the Kensington Kitten and Neuter Cat Club Show.

choice, as the procedure is much the same as at other shows, and it makes a good introduction into the world of show cats, with the opportunity to meet and talk to other fanciers, and to compare your own with other kittens.

About three months before, having decided on a show, write to the show manager for a schedule, enclosing a large stamped self-addressed envelope. It may seem a long time before the show to ask for a schedule, but a show manager has to get the catalogue ready for the printer several weeks before the show, involving checking all the entries, sending copy to the printer and going through the proof before it is finally printed. It is not necessary to belong to the club which is running the show, but there are advantages in doing so. The fees are usually slightly lower for members and there will be the special classes put on by the club for their members only. There is also the chance to win a cup, or wins on cups, and other prizes.

When the schedule arrives, it should be read through very carefully. Some show rules actually affecting the show are included in the schedule. However, the GCCF do publish a full set at £1, and if intending to go in for showing seriously it is advisable to know them all, as failure to comply with them may lead to disqualification. An exhibitor entering an Exemption Show should not worry too much; as long as the entry form is filled in correctly, with

the details required exactly as given on the registration or transfer form, and the classes chosen with care. Most shows insist that an exhibit is entered in at least four classes and not more than twelve, but for a first show and a young kitten four classes is plenty. The owner will have an opportunity to see how the kitten reacts at being shown, and can decide whether to show again or not. The most important class is the open or breed class which is for same variety exhibits. At the larger shows the kitten open classes may be divided into various ages, for example 3–5 and 5–9 months, but at the small shows may be for 3–9 months. At 9 months a kitten becomes a cat and can enter in the adult classes. Other classes could be Debutante for an exhibit that has not been shown at other GCCF shows; Maiden for one that has not won a first, second or third prize; Novice for one that has not won a first prize; and, if a member of the club, the Club Kitten class. There are other classes too, depending on the variety. In addition to the fees payable for each class, there will also be a benching fee for the pen used at the show, and the cost of the pass into the show. Some shows charge a set amount for entering a show which includes all the above, but the cost is very much the same.

Fill in the form with care and check that the details you give are exactly as on the transfer form, otherwise it is possible that the kitten could be disqualified with the loss of any prizes won.

The smaller shows may offer single or double pens for penning. A single pen is 2 × 2 ft (60 × 60 cm), with the double being 3 or 4 ft × 2 ft (90 or 120 cm × 60 cm). It is inadvisable to take a double for a small kitten, as it may crouch in the corner and may be difficult for the steward to reach. A double pen is ideal for a large male, but there are very few of them, and at the large shows they are usually kept for litters.

The open or breed class is a little more expensive than the other classes referred to as the miscellaneous and the club classes put on by other clubs for their members only. Some shows have specific club classes for their members only, and do not accept classes from other clubs.

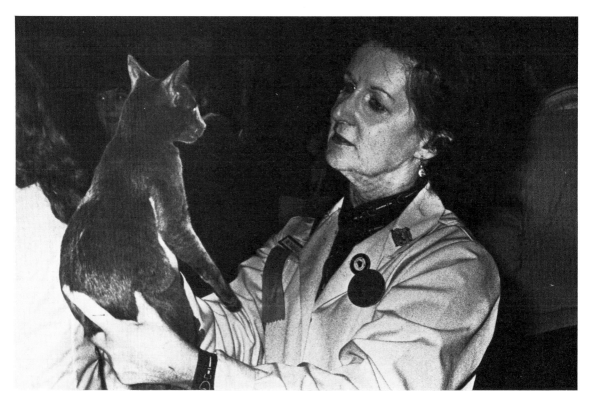

Judging a shorthaired Blue at the Notts & Derby Cat Show.

A few do have classes from the breed clubs and others from most of the clubs. If interested in a particular variety it is as well to belong to that breed club and so be able to enter their classes.

When sending in the entry form with the correct monies due, it is as well to enclose a stamped addressed card to be returned by the show manager to say that your entry has been accepted. You may also be asked to include a stamped self-addressed envelope for the tally and vetting-in card to be sent to you a week or two before the show. Some shows give out the tallies on the morning of the show. The tally will bear a number which will correspond with the pen in the show hall provided for your exhibit. It is impossible to send out the tallies until the entries close and the catalogue numbers can be allocated. Post your entry as soon as possible and do not wait for the closing date, as the hall may be full before if it is a very popular show.

Once you have heard that your entry has been accepted, it is important to spend more time on the animal's presentation, so that it looks beautiful on the day. You must have a cat basket or a cat box, as no exhibit is allowed into the show hall in one's arms or on a lead, and has to be in an escape-proof container.

There will be an early start in the morning with the vetting-in taking place from 7.30 am until 9.30 am. Every exhibit has to be examined by the veterinary surgeon before being allowed to be taken to its pen. Should there be any signs of fleas in the fur, running eyes, dirty ears, swollen gums or high temperature, or the animal looks out of condition, it will not be passed by the vet, and all the fees paid will be forfeit. In adult cats, a male would be turned away if he was a monorchid, that is having only one testicle, and a female cat obviously in kitten would also be disqualified. A hospital room is provided at all shows for such exhibits, but it is far better for the animal to be taken home rather than stay in the sick bay all day. It may be only

The Sealpoint Siamese Cat Club Show — a small and very successful show.

that the journey has caused an upset, but the vet has to think about all the exhibits, and not pass an animal that seems off-colour. Should there be any signs of an illness a week or more before the show, a certificate should be provided by the vet. This should be sent to the show manager, as it may be possible to get part of the fees paid returned.

The night before the show have ready the following:

1) The tally and white tape to go around the neck.
2) White litter tray.
3) Cotton wool and mild disinfectant.
4) Litter.
5) Hot water bottle (to be placed under the blanket if the hall is very cold).

Vetting-in at the Surrey & Sussex Show.

Vetting-in at the National Cat Club Show.

6) Clean warm white blanket to go in the pen.
7) White food dishes and food. Feeding is allowed after 1 pm.
8) Brush and comb.
9) Talcum powder in case of an accident – *Not* to be used in hall.
10) Vetting-in card, numbered tally, entry pass.
11) Schedule with classes marked for checking.
12) Drinking water must be in the pen all day. It is possible to buy a hook-on dish to go on the side of the pen, and which will not spill.
13) The basket.

On the morning of the show, do not forget the *cat*. This has happened before now with the husband thinking that the wife has put the cat

General view of the National Cat Club Show at Olympia.

Judging Best in Show at the Longhaired Cat Show, Chelsea.

in the basket, and vice versa.

Once past the veterinary surgeon, find the pen with the same number as the tally. Give the pen a quick wipe down with the cotton wool and disinfectant before putting in the blanket, litter tray, etc. Last of all if necessary give the animal a quick grooming and put in the pen. Most halls are cleared about 10 am with the exhibitors being allowed back about 12.30 pm. Some halls have a gallery from where the judging can be seen. The National Cat Club Show has the public in all day, which can make judging a little difficult with the crowds milling around.

The judge with her steward, both wearing white overalls, and with a trolley or small table, go to each pen as per the numbers given for the class in the judging book. The steward gets the exhibit out and places it on the table for the judge to examine. She will write her comments in her judging book, and the slips will be torn out and sent up to the awards table, and one slip will be put on the award board.

Once you are able to buy a catalogue you should check that the details printed are correct, and that your cat is entered in the right classes. Should there be anything wrong, it should be pointed out to the workers on the award table or platform. Prize cards start to go up on the pens and the animal may be fed.

If there is a Best in Show, the judges submit the numbers of their best cat, kitten and neuter, and later in the afternoon the panels sit to

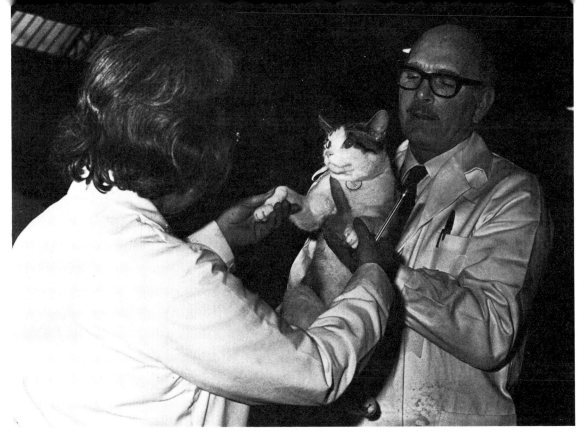

Judging the Pet Class at the National Cat Club Show, Olympia.

Studying the award list.

choose the best. At the large shows there will be a longhaired panel, a shorthaired panel, a Burmese panel and a Siamese panel. The judges on the panels will choose the best cat, kitten and neuter in each section, and if required to do so will choose the Best Cat, Kitten and Neuter to be Best in Show. Neuters do not compete against adult cats and kittens.

Rosettes and prize money are given out on the day and must be collected at the show. The catalogue is checked by the GCCF and if any of the entries and details given are wrong, disqualification may follow, and any winnings and rosettes must be returned.

Most shows close about 5.30 pm when everything may be packed up and the animal taken home, where for a few days it should be isolated from any other kittens or cats in the house. The owner will probably feel exhausted, but the kitten having been penned all day will probably feel full of life and rush madly about. It should be given a favourite meal and allowed to settle to sleep quietly.

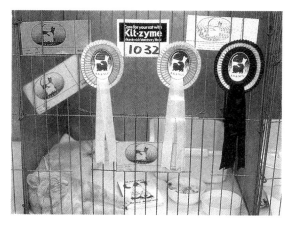

Show rosettes and cards on the pen.

NORTH AMERICA

Shows and showing in North America differ in many ways from those in Great Britain. To begin with there are eight registering bodies, each with a number of associated clubs. They vary in size considerably with the Cat Fanciers' Association (CFA) being the largest with clubs in every State in the USA and also in Canada and Japan. Canada has one association, the Canadian Cat Association, Inc. Clubs near the International border have members from both countries and there is no restriction on showing, with many fanciers travelling regularly to shows in both countries. It is possible to register a cat with several associations and exhibit at their affiliated clubs' shows, but nearly all will accept cats that are CFA registered.

Throughout the Cat Fancy world the pre-show procedure is much the same. The cat must be registered and transferred to the new owner, and must have had the required inoculations. The premium blank and entry blank for the show should be sent for about two months before hand. The entry blank has to be filled in with the details as given on the registration form, and sent to the show manager with the correct money before the closing date, usually about four weeks ahead. There are not so many classes in which to enter, so the catalogue preparation does not take so long.

The shows may be for one or two days, but there is a tendency at the moment to cut down on the expenses for the smaller shows by running one-day shows only.

There may be two, three or even four shows all being held in conjunction with the all-breed club running the show, and it is possible for the same cat to be entered in more than one of these shows, that is in a Specialist or Breed Club's class and in an All-breed Class and so on. There will be a judge for each show, working in her or his separate ring.

An exhibit that has not won before has to enter in the Novice class, whereas the Open class is for cats that may have won a prize or two, but have not yet had enough wins or points to be qualified to enter the Champion class. The Champion class is only for cats that have qualified. Points are given for each Champion beaten, and eventually a cat may become a Grand Champion. It is possible for a cat in the novice class to win, and to go up into the Open, and if still unbeaten to go into the Champion class. The points required to become a Grand Champion do vary in the different associations,

American method of judging at the River City Cat Show, Texas.

but the number required in the CFA affiliated clubs' shows is high, and it would require a very large number of Champions at one show for a cat to start as a Novice and finish up as a Grand Champion on the same day. The points, however, may be carried on to another show.

The classes are divided into male and female, breed and colour. There are similar classes for the altered cats, that is the neuter male and spayed females (Novice, Open, Premier and Grand Premier).

The adult classes are for cats over eight months, and the kitten classes for kittens 4–8 months old. there are also classes for household pets which must be altered and at least 8 months old. They have their own judge, and a red and white merit ribbon may be given to each pet considered worthy. They are judged on condition and personality, and usually appear in very attractive decorated pens for which prizes may be given.

The kitten classes are judged first, and First, Second and Third prizes are awarded. Clubs do not give prize money, but various ribbons, trophies and rosettes. The ribbons for the adults are the reverse colours to those of Britain in that the First is blue, the Second red, and the Third yellow. The First may also be given a red, white and blue winner's ribbon. The Best of Class may be given a black ribbon and the Second Best a

white ribbon. It was very difficult when I first judged in the States, as the judges have to put the ribbons on the cages themselves, and I had to be careful not to confuse the ribbons.

Once your cat has been accepted for the show, it is time to consider the decor of his cage, as all exhibits are allowed to have decorated cages as the judges do not go to them. The curtains may be chosen to enhance the cat's colouring, as may the cage floor cover, the litter tray, the toys and food bowl. The whole show is very colourful, with drapes, the attractive decorated cages, flowers and often flags hanging from the roof.

Each exhibit has to be vetted in and once passed may be taken to its assigned cage in the hall, and the owner can start preparing the cage. The cats are not penned in their different varieties, but an exhibitor may have all her cats penned next to one another, or may even ask to be put close to a friend's.

Each judge has a separate judging ring, with a table and chair, and behind them a row of undecorated cages, usually eight or ten, so that all the cats in one class can be placed there ready for her to start. At some shows owners take their cats to the cages, and at others special stewards do this. Seats are provided in front of the judges' tables for the exhibitors to watch the proceedings. Judging starts at 10 am and the show may go on until 7 pm. The judge herself takes the cat out of the cage and places it on the table, giving it a thorough examination comparing it with the standard required for that particular breed. While doing this she may tell the audience what she is looking for, and will then replace it in the cage. She will make notes in her judging book or a clerk may do this for her. The judge will disinfect her hands and the table top before taking the next cat out, until she has handled all the cats in that class.

When I was judging there I was given a peacock feather which rather amused me, but I was told it was to attract the cat's attention and to make them look up. It was certainly a good idea to make them open their eyes and to see the eye colour. The cats too seemed to think it was just a lovely game.

American judge examining a Birman for Best in Show.

After the judge has made up her mind as to which are the prizewinners, she will take the appropriate ribbon and put it on the winner's cage. She will do the same for the second and the third, and the cats will be taken back to their own cages, but the winner remains behind and is included in the class's judging. The cats come up for the next class, and all are judged. If the judge considers her first winner beats all the cats in this class, the Open, it will remain to compete against the Champions in the next class. If beaten it is returned to its own cage. If the best cat it will be awarded points according to the number of Champions beaten, and which will count towards a Grand Championship, should it win that class. It would not be able to bear that title until it had the large number of points required, but these can be carried over to other shows.

In the meantime judging will be going on in other rings, and the same cat will be needed for judging for them if entered in the other shows. If a cat is really outstanding it will be possible for it to win in those as well, but a cat can win under one judge and be given nothing by another.

The unbeaten cats, kittens and altered cats go forward to the high spot of the show, the Best of the Best, invariably judged by a famous judge.

The judges do not wear overalls as in Britain and really dress up for the occasion. In fact, I was told by a horrified steward that I could not possibly appear in my ring wearing a white overall. I was fascinated by the judging of the best by a male judge, who was immaculately dressed in a red blazer, with tie to match, and very smartly cut trousers. First he walked slowly up and down the line of unbeaten prizewinning cats from all the rings, and examined them on his table, while the waiting crowd held their breath. He would have one cat out, put it back, take another out, put it back, and then perhaps get a steward to hold one while he held the other. Both were replaced and he again studied the row of very beautiful cats, all on their best behaviour. He took the winner's ribbon in his hand, went slowly along the row again amid dead silence, paused before one, and I could feel the tension building up, as he placed the ribbon on the pen of another cat altogether. There was loud applause and the fortunate owner burst into tears. In the end he chose the five best cats, i.e. the Best, the Second Best, the Third Best, and so on. The five best kittens and the five best altered cats were chosen in the same way.

In North America, unlike in Britain, judges are paid a little for each cat or kitten they judge. They are given travel expenses, and one or two nights at a hotel, dependent as to whether it is a one- or two-day show. The judges can cost a show a great deal of money, as a judge may come from Canada to judge in the Southern states, or vice versa. There are all-breed judges and specialist judges, and all have to attend special classes and pass examinations before they can become judges. With so many shows in the States and Canada, it is possible for a judge to go to a show nearly every weekend, and also for exhibitors to show their cats as often as they can afford. By showing in both countries a cat can become eventually an International Grand Champion, and a neuter an International Grand Premier.

AUSTRALIA AND NEW ZEALAND

There are many opportunities for exhibiting in Australia, as the seven States, Northern Territory, Queensland, South Australia, Victoria, Tasmania, New South Wales and Western Australia, all have their own Governing Councils and Cat Fancies, each having many affiliated cat clubs. A number of the shows are held under the auspices of the Royal Agricultural Society, and some clubs hold two or three shows a year, with the smallest being in Alice Springs right in the centre of the continent. There is a Co-ordinating Council of Australia which seeks to do just that between the various Cat Fancies.

As in North America and Britain, cats have to be registered and transferred to a new owner weeks before the show date, and have had the necessary inoculations. The schedule should be sent for at least two months before the show, filled in correctly, and sent to the show manager promptly.

There are a good choice of classes in the schedule, with open classes for each variety, including Shaded Silver, which is an old variety, once recognised in Britain. As in America, the Colourpoints are known as Himalayans. The miscellaneous classes may include Breeders, Limit, Novice, Australian-bred Cats and Kittens, State-bred Cats and Kittens, and maybe Personality and Best-groomed Classes. Some shows have classes for kittens under three months, which are not allowed in Britain. The classes do vary from State to State, but the rules and regulations are much the same for all shows.

Fanciers tend to show mostly at local shows, but the large Royal Agricultural Society's shows attract a large attendance, and the shows are held in conjunction with many other events, including show jumping, dog shows, sheep-shearing and so on.

Judging tends to start about 9.30 am and should finish about 1.30 pm when the public are admitted. The system of judging is as in Britain, with the judge and steward going to the cages, with a small trolley. Some shows are trying ring judging, but it is not general as yet. There is a panel of judges to pick the Best in Show cats, but to avoid carrying cats through the crowds the judges are given a list of the exhibits nominated and go to their cages, and each judge chooses the ones he or she prefers, and informs the show manager. The cats or kittens with a majority vote win, but if there are really some outstanding exhibits it is frequently a unanimous decision. Some shows in England and Scotland do judge the Best in Show in the same way.

There are shows going on all through the year, with judges sometimes having to fly thousands of miles to them, perhaps judging one week in Melbourne and the next week in Darwin. There is an interchange of judges between the separate States, and all judges have to attend training courses and sit strict examinations. British judges are invited frequently, with their opinions being much valued. As the expense is so great, usually about six clubs will share the cost, with various exhibitors as hosts.

Australian fanciers do import cats from Britain and New Zealand, and a few from the States. They have quarantine, but it is matter of weeks only for cats from Britain and none from New Zealand. Whereas once the cats from Britain had to come by ship, taking many weeks, and being looked after by the crew, now they fly often on special flights.

Both North and South Islands of New Zealand have a very flourishing Cat Fancy under the same central council, the Governing Council of New Zealand. The shows are run very similarly to those in Australia and Britain, and British judges as well as Australian are often invited judge there. The New Zealand judges do attend special courses and have to take examinations. The standard of the pedigree cats is high, and many are exported to Australia. They are sent over by plane and there are no quarantine restrictions.

8 Cat Care

By James Allcock MRCVS

Many years ago Daniel Defoe penned some lines about the 'True-born Englishman', but he could have been writing about cats:

> Great families of yesterday we show
> And Lords whose parents were the Lord knows who.

The majority of cats seen at shows are from 'great families of yesterday' and have an impressive pedigree, but well-loved cats, 'whose parents were the Lord knows who', compete in the Household Pet Sections. Pedigree or not, choosing the right kitten is the first and most important step in preparing for any cat's show career; and it is just as important if you are looking for a kitten to join your family – and perhaps go to just the odd show or two.

A cat is forever, so spend time choosing. Decide on the breed that you want. Never, never underestimate the time (and devotion) that is involved in keeping a longhaired cat groomed so that he looks and feels respectable. If you think that a good combing the day before a show is all that is really needed, believe me, it is not.

Decide which sex of cat you prefer. Perhaps you have decided that whatever the sex it will be neutered, but there is a difference in temperament between neutered males (bold, brash and big) and spayed females (more fastidious, gentler, somewhat smaller). If you have an ambition to breed, and perhaps to produce a champion of the future, your choice must be a female kitten as a household cat. I know it 'takes two to Tango', and one of each sort to breed, but a tomcat, unneutered, does not make a good house pet. They are delightful characters, but when spring comes around every tom worthy of the name sets off on his travels with one idea in his mind – and when he achieves his ambition he does not wait to collect any stud fee to pay you for his keep throughout the rest of the year. Pedigree stud toms must be confined during the breeding season at least. Every entire male cat has the distinctive tomcat smell which permeates any house that he lives in.

Once the breed, sex and perhaps colour is sorted out, the source is the next important decision. Always get a kitten from the home he was born into. Change of home at seven or eight weeks of age is a stressful experience for any kitten. If he goes to a pet shop or cat's home at seven weeks of age, and then moves again to you at eight weeks, these two changes of diet and environment might be too much, and an upset, unwell kitten results. Look for a breeder near to your home, or within easy driving distance at least. There is a strange idea that any pedigree kitten from the other end of the country must be better than a locally bred one.

Try to find the kitten that is to be yours when he is two or three weeks old – and there is no harm in choosing, provisionally at least, before a kitten is born. If mother cat is the breed and colour that you are looking for then a 'keep for me' label on an unborn kitten is quite appropriate.

Seven to eight weeks is the right age to change homes. This is young enough to allow a kitten to learn to socialise with humans. Some breeders insist that nine to twelve weeks is better. The kitten is older, so there is less stress, they argue. This is true, as far as physical upset is concerned, but a twelve-week-old kitten that has stayed with Mum and his litter mates has begun to socialise with cats – not humans. If one pet cat is going to enjoy living with you, and you with him, the cat should become accustomed to human company at an early age. Most

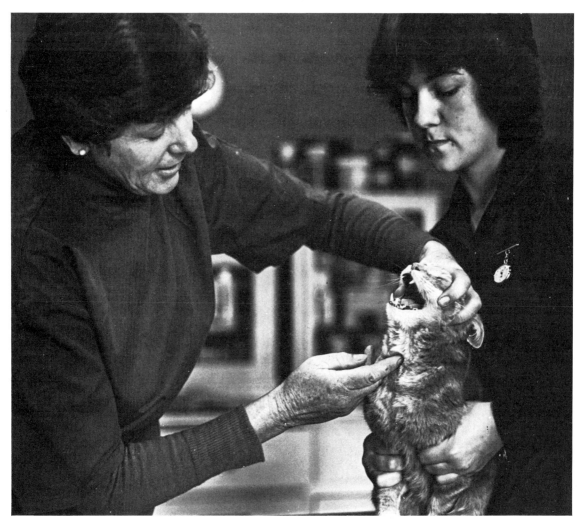

A vet examining a cat's mouth.

of the physical stress can be avoided if kittens are introduced to solid food from four weeks of age, so that leaving mother and moving to a diet of cat food at seven weeks is no great and sudden change. Try to persuade the breeder of your kitten to offer a little canned food when the litter reaches four weeks of age. (Grace Pond and Mary Dunnill cannot agree with the ages given here for selling kittens, and point out that it is a strong recommendation by the Governing Council of the Cat Fancy that no pedigree kittens are sold under the age of thirteen weeks. Registered breeders abide by this recommendation.)

Although you might have reserved a kitten before he was born there comes a day when you have to make the positive decision that *this* kitten is to be *the* one. Look very closely and choose with a cold heart. You want to start with a healthy kitten, physically perfect. Here is a check list.

1) *Nose*. This should be clean, even-shaped, both nostrils the same size, no discharge, no sneezing.
2) *Teeth*. They should meet evenly; at this age

they will be baby teeth and every tooth that you see now will be lost and replaced by the time the kitten is six months old. They should be in the right alignment now.

3) *Eyes*. Look for clean, bright eyes that are wide open. There should not be any excess tears or discharges. Do not believe it if you are told that 'it's the sawdust', or 'just a bit of cold in the eye, cold tea will cure it'. Messy eyes could be the prelude to all sorts of troubles. Start with perfect ones.

4) *Ears*. Again, these should be clean. A dark brown wax in them may indicate ear mite infection. Easy to clear up, but the breeder of the cat should have seen to this, not started you off with a kitten with ear trouble. Lice, which should never be there, can be found around the ears. Kittens should not shake their heads – this is another sign of ear mites.

5) *Legs*. No lameness. A kitten of seven weeks of age is not a very elegant mover, but he should scamper about, not hold one paw up in the air whenever he stands still. Count the toes. There should be four on each foot, with a dew claw on the inside of the front legs. Some cats have extra toes. This disqualifies them from shows and the nails on supernumerary toes can overgrow and cause troubles throughout a cat's life.

6) *Coat*. This should be clean, free from lice, fleas or specks of black grit – which is probably flea dirt. Healthy kittens do not have to carry fleas, and cat-keeping does not mean flea-keeping is inevitable. There should not be any hairless patches either.

7) *The rear end*. It is not indelicate to inspect this part of a kitten. Look under the tail. There should be no signs of diarrhoea nor any redness or soreness. Check the sex of the kitten at this end. 'She had such a pretty face', is not a reliable method of sexing. Experienced breeders can be relied upon to sort out the sexes for you, but if you are in doubt distance is the guide. The distance between the anus and the next visible opening is greatest in the male.

8) *Mother and the rest of the litter*. All other cats on the premises should appear healthy. If there are sneezes, sore eyes, or diarrhoea in a number of cats, the kitten that you choose could be the next to succumb. So buy from kennels where every cat is in rude health.

There is one other check that should be made but seven or eight weeks old might be too soon. Be certain that a tom kitten has both testicles descended and in the scrotum. This development fails in a few cats. If one testicle only is descended the animal is described as a monorchid; if both fail to descend this is a cryptorchid. In neither instance can the cat be shown. It is most unwise to breed from a monorchid because there is some evidence that the defect is an inherited one. A cryptorchid is infertile because a retained testicle, still in the abdomen, is at too high a temperature to allow normal sperm development. Normal sex hormones are developed by cryptorchid cats so they wander and smell just as any fully fertile tom. Castration is quite possible, and essential if they are to live as part of the family, but it is a much more complex and therefore more expensive operation in the imperfect male cat than in the normal one.

After all those checkpoints you might feel like someone who has just read a medical encyclopaedia, and is suffering from mental indigestion. If you are doubtful of your own ability to 'vet' your potential show winner it is not unreasonable to ask your vet to examine a kitten before you actually complete the purchase. The odd old-fashioned breeder might resent this check on his/her stock. Good breeders welcome it because they are confident that nothing wrong will be found.

You have decided on *the* kitten and you want to hurry home with it, but you must slow down again. Ask the breeder if it has been wormed (kittens should be wormed at about six weeks of age). Make certain that you have the pedigree as well as the kitten. If you are paying for a pedigree kitten a part of the cost is that piece of paper. Do not be put off with 'I'll send it on', sometimes people remember to bank your cheque but forget to post the pedigree. Find out which food the kitten has been weaned onto. It is possible that some vaccinations have been done already. The usual age for these injections is twelve weeks but some catteries do immunise

A plastic cat igloo.

kittens from six weeks of age. If your kitten has had such injections make certain that you collect the certificate so that if further injections are due you are able to tell your vet precisely what has been given beforehand.

Perhaps you will be told that the kitten is from feline-leukaemia-tested parents and wonder what this means. There is a leukaemia that affects cats and is caused by a virus. Blood testing can indicate if a cat colony is infected or not and some breeders test for this. It is not a guarantee that your kitten could never become infected, but it does indicate that the human parents of your new kitten are taking every care possible. Now it is time to leave with the kitten. You have bought a cat carrier, I trust. The good ones are costly but it is worthwhile and as this kitten is going to be with you for at least fourteen years £20 plus for the basket is not too much. I prefer the plastic or plastic-coated metal mesh carrying cages to the wicker ones. There

are three reasons for this. Most cats like to know where they are going and travel contentedly if they can see out. Plastic, or metal covered in plastic, is easy to clean. Anyone who has tried to clean a wicker basket after a diarrhoeic cat has had an accident knows the difficulties presented by a woven floor. Many wicker baskets have an ill-fitting door, held by leather strap hinges, and able-bodied cats find little difficulty in escaping.

Avoid the temptation to fill the basket with soft bedding and blankets. Paper, possibly newspaper, is the best covering for the carrier floor. It is clean, sterile from a cat disease aspect, easy to obtain and easy to dispose of by burning. Blankets, sheets and cushions need washing – and do not always get it – and they can occupy a lot of space. I have seen many a cat basket so full of soft cushions that there is barely room for the cat; he must have come out with a very stiff neck, because he had to travel in a head down, praying position once the lid was closed upon him. There is one newspaper disadvantage with white or very light-coloured cats. The print can come off and make the cat look very grubby, so unprinted paper is best for these colours. (I do not believe that the printer's ink is in any way harmful to cats in the quantities that can come off a printed sheet; it is just messy.)

Home at last. His first introduction to a new world. A properly brought-up kitten is curious, confident and eager to find out. Let him. If there are other pets already in residence the new kitten should meet them as soon as possible. There will be hisses and spats, but noises do not hurt. The key to successful introductions is to leave it to the animals. Be there to interfere in a serious crisis, and, most important of all, arrange it so that either animal can make an honourable retreat. Real fights, real injuries, occur when your old cat or dog has to defend his territory against this new interloper. If he could have sidled out through the door, gone to rest behind the settee or if the new kitten had somewhere to hide so that eyeball-to-eyeball conflict was avoided, then so would the fights be avoided. Cardboard boxes are useful places of retreat and make a very good kitten bed. Place the box on its side, with the opening towards the wall. Newspaper makes the best box lining. The kitten can go into the box (and he will), there is a roof over his head, and he is facing the wall so that there is a high degree of privacy. The new kitten can hide and feel safe. The old cat does not have to notice and can pretent that the kitten does not exist. Honour is satisfied. Amicable relationships almost always develop between the new and old pets, but it might take three months before all is sweetness and light.

As soon as the kitten realises that this new household provides food, he has a very strong reason for settling down. My cats live on good quality canned cat food, and I see no reason for making cat feeding more complicated than manipulating a tin-opener. Let the makers of the food worry about vitamins, minerals, and essential amino-acids. Good quality canned food has the correct quantities of all these elements included. The very few cases of diet-induced

disease that one sees in cats are almost always the result of allowing a cat to dictate his choice of food. The 'all liver or I'll sulk' cat with an indulgent owner will develop a very painful arthritis as a result of Vitamin A excess and calcium deficiency. When that cat is forced to eat a properly balanced diet he recovers – and would never have suffered the pain if his owner had been stronger-minded.

A kitten of eight weeks needs four meals a day. Make the last meal at night the largest one – a full tummy is conducive to sleep. How much to feed is partly judgment, but as a guide, a 400-gm (14-oz) can should last a ten-week-old kitten about three days. Each meal should be eaten within ten minutes. Do not leave uneaten food about. The kitten learns that it is always there and becomes a miserable feeder. If there are other animals in the house, food can be a source of quarrels. The 'dog in the manger' attitude applies to cats also, and if later in life your kitten is to use a cat door saucers of uneaten food invite visits from hungry wandering cats. There are canned foods specially formulated for young growing kittens, somewhat more expensive than the ordinary foods. They are more concentrated and perhaps a kitten might grow a bit better if fed this way, but my kittens have always done very well on the ordinary adult grade food.

At four months of age one of the meals can be cut out, and as the kitten approaches six months two meals per day are sufficient. The kitten's own feeding behaviour will usually tell you which meal is best omitted. He may be enthusiastic about food at every meal time, but there will be some obvious preference. In very hot weather adult cats may not be keen on food during the heat of the day and even a six-month-old kitten can appear non-hungry at 4 pm when the temperature is in the high 80s F, yet ravenous at dusk when conditions are bearable again.

All animals need fluid as well as food and cats are no exception, although many cats seem to drink little. Ordinary meat contains around 70 per cent moisture and so does canned food. So cats take the majority of their fluid in the food when they eat. Water or milk should be available so that the cat can 'top up' if he is thirsty. Some cats – particularly Siamese and Burmese – seem to have an aversion to milk and will drink nothing except water. I think they are right. Cow's milk is an unnatural food for a cat and sometimes too much milk can be a cause of chronic diarrhoea. Lactose, which is the sugar in milk, is not broken down during digestion and this substance in the lower part of the bowel means that too many, too loose, motions result. Moderation in all things is a good maxim, so not too much milk and none at all if bowel activity is excessive.

Dry cat food is also available. These are compounded foods so that all the necessary nutrients are there, but very little fluid (7 per cent on average). This means that the cat has to obtain almost all his fluid by drinking and a few cats do not drink enough to make up for the water that is not in the food. Thus their urine becomes very concentrated and salts in the urine may crystalline out to form a sandy, gravelly type material that is intensely irritant to the lining of the bladder. Cystitis is caused, which is painful in the female cat and life-endangering in the male, because the tiny bladder stones can block the urethra and prevent him passing urine. Every packet of dried cat biscuits has a message printed on it about providing fresh milk or water at all times. The cat cannot read the instructions, and some owners do not, but they are important. Cats like the 'crunchiness' of dry food and the hard biscuits help to clean and polish the teeth. Dry food is not really suitable for young kittens, but adult cats do very well on it. Nevertheless, if a cat has ever suffered from any bladder trouble it is unwise to feed this type of food to that particular animal. Perhaps the best of both worlds is to feed canned food for most of the cat's needs and a few dry cat biscuits each day to clean and polish the teeth. My cats make do by stealing the dog's biscuits to use as their tooth brush and, if the noise they make crunching them into powder is anything to go by, thoroughly enjoy the jaw exercise.

Especially with longhairs, if you have no

Grass is essential in preventing hairballs, especially in longhairs.

garden, provide a pot of grass for the cat to eat. This will prevent the formation of hairballs in the digestive system, as it acts as an emetic.

Whatever goes in must come out, which introduces the subject of toilet training. Cats always intend to be clean – by their standards. Training consists of directing their natural instincts of cleanliness so that the cat behaviour coincides with our, human, ideas. How you train depends to an extent on what you wish to achieve and how your house is organised. One thing is certain, training by punishment or telling off after an accident is totally ineffective. Teach the cat what *to do* rather than what *not to do*. If you want to train him to use the great outdoors, then I suggest that you start, even at eight weeks, to indicate that outside is the right place. This might mean keeping a litter tray just outside the back door. If the weather is wet, keep the tray in a waterproof box – an old tea chest on its side or something like an old-fashioned dog kennel. This will keep the litter dry and gives the kitten a degree of privacy and security. The great outdoors must be a little frightening for a tiny kitten. He feels very vulnerable while he is digging a hole and concentrating, so dry litter to dig in attracts him, and walls around and a roof over his head mean that he does not have to worry about an enemy cat attacking while he is defenceless. By taking the kitten outdoors you are teaching him that this is the right place. If he is to use a tray indoors the same routine of pointing in the right direction applies. Frequently renewed litter encourages the kitten; a smelly tray is as repulsive to them as it is to us. Almost every kitten should be totally clean by twelve weeks of age and many are without mistake from the very first day – if the owner is co-operative in providing the facilities.

When your kitten first joins you he has to learn many things; he will learn how to behave

and how to react whether you teach him or not. He might learn to resent being combed, and learn that if he struggles you stop combing him, so he has won that battle of wills. He might learn that if he looks hungrily at the fridge you will weaken and a small piece of the Sunday joint is provided. Very much better for all if he learns that you are in charge and you make the decisions. Early lessons are the most effective.

Handling a cat is easiest if the cat is placed on a table, which has a smooth surface. The cat cannot get a grip to help his struggles, and the human is working at a convenient and natural height. Vetting-in at a show involves the cat being examined while he is on a table. So one early lesson is to put your kitten on a smooth-topped table and comb him. An eight-week-old shorthaired kitten hardly needs to see a comb, but he should learn that combing happens, it is not very unpleasant, and the sooner he behaves

Cream Burmese using a litter tray.

Grooming a shorthaired cat with a rubber brush.

well the sooner he can go about his own affairs again.

While he is on the table look into his ears, and his eyes. Open his mouth, look under his tail, lie him on his back and look at his tummy. Part game, part training, but all this will happen to him at his first show, and if he is a well-behaved cat the vet will give him full marks if no one else does. Even if the kitten never gets to a show in

Opposite: The finishing touches.

Grooming the underside of a longhaired Blue.

his life, this early handling can save trouble later on. When, or if, he develops ear trouble at three years old, you may have to put drops in his ears. The trained kitten is likely to be better treated, the drops reach the right place more easily, and the ears recover quickly. The untrained, uncontrolled cat can be untreated because the owner finds administration of drops, pills or eye ointment too difficult.

An introduction to bathing is worthwhile before too much time has passed; if your kitten is longhaired and light-coloured, washing him, and making him fit to be shown, will occupy a significant amount of time. The sooner the pair of you reach agreement as to who is to win the battles of the bath, the better. Hair driers help afterwards; thus a kitten should learn that the buzzing noise is totally harmless and grown up cats do not panic.

When you collected your kitten you were told to keep him at home until he had been vaccinated, if this had not already been done. The reason for this important precaution is to prevent the kitten meeting infection before inoculation had made him develop an immunity. It is wise to allow the kitten to settle in his new home for a fortnight or so before injecting him, so that the stress of changing homes has

passed and he can concentrate on developing good immunity after vaccination.

There are two major diseases that every cat should be protected against: feline enteritis and cat 'flu. There are at least a dozen different vaccines available and the detailed advice about which to use for your kitten must come from your own vet. In general, vaccination involves two injections, two, three or four weeks apart. The age of the kitten and the type of vaccine govern the interval. Most of the vaccines are given by injection, but the 'flu protection can be achieved by instilling drops into the cat's nose. When the course of injections is complete your vet will give you a certificate to that effect. Read this before you leave the surgery. Make sure that the details are complete and that you know when the booster vaccination is due. Immunity does not last for ever and boosters — and a completed certificate — are an annual (usually) ritual. Keep the certificate in a safe place. You will need to take it to shows, and most reputable kennels insist on an up-to-date certificate before they will take your cat for boarding.

There might be a fortnight to wait before injections, but telephone your vet very soon after getting the kitten and ask his advice about and routine of vaccination. Also prepare the

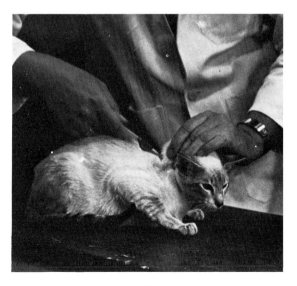

Siamese cat being vaccinated.

130

kitten. Showing and visiting the veterinary surgery both involve travelling. Take the kitten for a few rides in the car, in his travelling basket; do not leave him in a stationary car in hot weather, but the odd trip, even every day while he is young will get him used to, and bored by, car journeys. Frightened cats salivate excessively; panic-stricken cats can produce from the other end of the digestive tract too. Unhandled, untrained, untravelled cats sometimes arrive at their first show wet, dirty, smelly and extremely unattractive. Make certain that yours turns up clean and tidy, full of his own importance and enjoying every minute of it.

He will enjoy his visit to the vet too, so take advantage of the reflected glory from your kitten to find out about neutering – if that is to be. Each vet has his own preferred time for this operation. Around six to nine months is the most usual age. Planning ahead never hurts, so find out now, and if you have a female cat and hope to breed from her, talk to your vet about heat control in that period of time before you take her to stud. A queen on heat can be very noisy, becomes an expert escape artist and manages to mate with a most unsuitable swain because he just happened to be passing. There are injections and tablets that can prevent heat for some time.

At any cat show controlled by the rules of the Governing Council of the Cat Fancy every cat has to be examined by one of the veterinary surgeons appointed to that show, and will not be admitted unless the cat is passed fit and suitable. Vets are looking for any infections that could affect other cats, as well as fleas, lice, mange and ringworm as external troubles. Infectious colds, eye infections and mouth ulcers are some of the general signs that lead to rejection from the show. By the very nature of a show, when hundreds, and often thousands, of cats have to be seen in a couple of hours, the 'vetting-in' is a screening examination – and nonetheless valuable for that. Anything suspicious must stay out. As well as infections we are looking for some defects that might be inherited – extra claws, or signs that they have

been removed. Declawing of a normal cat also disqualifies it, and quite rightly too. It should disqualify the owner in my view. I cannot accept that such an operation is ever justified no matter how valuable the furniture. Do not keep a cat if the three-piece suite is so precious – but that is an aside.

The final job that the vet has to do is count – with tomcats at least. Normal testicle development is essential for a show cat – which explains why, when selecting a kitten, the right numbers of claws and other things are so important. Do not panic about vetting-in. Remember the vaccination certificates, do not leave your entry card in the car, turn up with a clean, flea-free, healthy cat, well trained and well behaved; you will impress the vet, perhaps captivate the judges, but, most important of all, the *cat* will enjoy his day out.

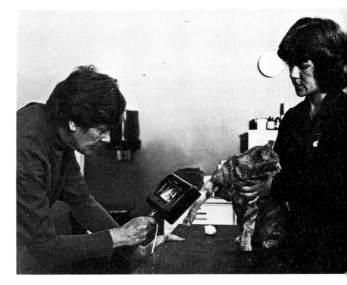

A vet examining a cat for ringworm with a 'woods lamp'.

9 The Cat in Commerce

In Ancient Egypt where it is thought that cats were first domesticated thousands of years ago, they were most certainly involved in commerce. Skilled craftsmen were employed by the owners of their revered cats to make golden ear rings or collars of gold for them to wear. Delightful necklaces and bracelets made of rows of tiny figures of cats were made as gifts for children. Amulets depicting cats and models of cats were produced in their thousands. Even after death the small bodies were embalmed, wrapped in expensive linen or cotton, and placed in beautifully decorated mummy cases, made of wood or bronze, even in sculptured stone, often ornamented with gold leaf. Artists painted murals showing cats, and musical instruments such as sistrums, which were used in processions to pay homage to the cat goddess, Pasht, frequently had cat models on them. All these must have provided employment for many, and today much of their work is sought after by collectors, sometimes fetching very large sums.

Cats were thought to have been introduced into Britain by the Romans, whose legions may have carried banners and ensigns depicting cats. The Romans left, but the cats remained, and in AD 948 Prince Howel the Good made laws protecting cats; giving the worth of a kitten before it opened its eyes as a penny, a large sum in those days, and once it had caught a mouse two pence. Anyone who stole or killed a cat was fined a sheep and a lamb, or as much wheat to cover the cat when held up by the tail with the nose just touching the ground, which was quite a lot of very expensive corn.

CAT FOOD

Cat food has always played a big part in cats and commerce. Dr Johnson fed his cat on oysters, which is not as exotic as it sounds, as they were very cheap in his day. Later when the cats' meat man came along, with the increased popularity of the cat, many horses were bought and sold for cat meat, which was very sad for the horses, but must have meant considerable employment at the end of the Victorian era. Carriers delivered meat to various parts of the country, and hundreds, if not thousands of men sold the cats' meat in the streets and markets, and went from house to house. This went on for several decades.

As long ago as the end of the seventeenth century some food for humans was preserved in glass jars, and later after years of experimentation cans began to be used. In the 1930s it was possible to buy in North America and Britain some food for pets in glass jars. It was then that Pedigree Petfoods came on the scene (under the name of Mars), and 'Chappie' appeared in the shops. It was looked on as dog food, but was frequently given to cats. Further experiments were carried out with the idea of producing pet foods in cans, but the 1939–45 War prohibited the use of metal to a certain extent. It was in the 1950s that thought was given once again to the canning of food for cats and dogs. Nobody could possibly have foreseen at that time what an enormous worldwide industry would result, involving modern technology, huge factories, machinery and other equipment, chemists, analysts, scientists, veterinary surgeons and a multitude of others working to produce and sell foods that appeal and also keep the animals in tip-top condition.

A number of other companies were also producing canned and dry cat foods. It is impossible to calculate how many are connected with the industry and its sideshoots, including

Above: Advertisement appearing on the back cover of *Our Cats*, December 20, 1902.

Right above: Modern techniques in the preparation of catfood (Pedigree Petfoods).

advertising agents producing commercials on television and advertising, and, going back to the cats' meat days, carriers and distributors, the shops that sell and the customers that buy.

SHOW ACCESSORIES

At the cat shows, too, in just a small way at first, commerce was involved, with pens being needed to exhibit the cats, drapings to go on the tabling, cat baskets and cat carriers of all kinds, feeding bowls, litter trays, small balls and toys of all descriptions, to mention just a few. As more people went in for pedigree cats, brushes, combs and powders were used more and more, and pet owners began to realise that their cats

The black cat motif was used by the Home Office in this recruitment poster, shown in *Our Cats*, September 1960.

Don't trust to luck

Train in

CIVIL DEFENCE

also needed grooming. Cat blankets, sleeping baskets and many sundries are now bought by the thousand.

MEDICINE

The pharmaceutical manufacturers, such as Burroughs Wellcome, spent many years in research and finally produced vaccines and inoculations to combat the killer illnesses that were rampant in the early days of the Cat Fancy. Over the years many medical preparations have been produced which are necessary to safeguard the health of a cat from worm tablets and flea powders to anaesthetics given in neutering and spaying.

SOUVENIRS

Many cat shows have stalls that sell almost everything connected with the cat world from heated sleeping bags, cat harnesses and collars, little houses for toilet purposes, litter and litter

Post Office Greetings Telegram reproduced in *Our Cats*, August 1960.

trays, brushes for getting rid of cats' hairs and other 'catty' articles.

FILMS AND TELEVISION

Cats appeared in the early film cartoons, Felix being the first, and later Tom and Jerry. Walt Disney was fond of having cats in his films, including *The Lady and the Tramp, That Darned Cat*, with Hayley Mills, and *The Cat from Outer Space*, featuring an Abyssinian. Cats nowadays act as models for commercials, not only for cat foods but also for carpets and new homes.

Jason, the Siamese cat of *Blue Peter* (see p. 40) was known all over the British Isles, and attracted many children when he appeared at many cat shows. When he died Jack and Jill took his place. Jill was a spotted Silver Tabby, and Jack a classic Silver Tabby. Unfortunately Jill died recently, but Jack is still on *Blue Peter* and comes to shows regularly.

Blue Peter Silver Tabbies, Jack and Jill, at the National Cat Club Show, Olympia.

CATTERIES

Cats cannot be left to fend for themselves when their owners are away, and if there are no friendly neighbours to help out, the answer is a boarding cattery. There are now many boarding catteries all over the country, some excellent, some not so good. It is most important for owners to inspect the premises before taking a cat there to ensure that the pens and runs where the animals are kept look clean, and the cats there already look happy. The charges vary considerably, but it is essential for the owner to use one that will make the cat comfortable and warm rather than to think of the money side, as the most expensive may not always be the one preferred.

PEDIGREE STOCK

Whereas once Blue Persian kittens were sold for three guineas if they were very good, the prices nowadays may well start at about £80 and up to more than £300 for an outstanding one. Stud fees too vary considerably, according to the male used, but breeding is not really a paying hobby, as the kittens have to be fed for three months or more, with inoculations and possibly other veterinary bills to pay.

BOOKS

One of the most interesting of early cat books is *The Book of the Cat*, written and illustrated by Chas. H. Ross, published in 1868 by Griffith and Farran at the Corner of St Paul's Churchyard. It is subtitled 'A Chit-Chat Chronicle of Feline Facts and Fancies, legendary, lyrical, medical, mirthful and miscellaneous'. It includes the information that black cats especially are said to be highly charged with electricity, which, when the animal is irritated, is easily visible in the dark! Then it gives directions for producing the effect. Harrison Weir's *Our Cats and All About Them* is a classic; Harrison Weir 'conceived the idea that it would be well to hold "Cat Shows" so that the different breeds, colours, markings etc. might be more carefully attended to', and with admirable speed he called up his friend, the Manager of the Crystal Palace, and in a few days 'presented my scheme in full working order'. In his book, he describes the various breeds, with his own pen and ink drawings and also gives Points of Excellence. Strangely enough, he gives no advice on preparation for showing, and we must turn to John Jennings and his book *Domestic and Fancy Cats*

to learn about 'the culminating feature of the fancier's ambition – exhibitions.' We find that Mr G. Billett, of Southampton, is the 'Father of exhibition pens and penning.' There are detailed instructions on preparation of the schedule, rules and regulations, and general management; a veritable 'Show Manager's Guide'.

The Book of the Cat by Frances Simpson, published by Cassell and Company Limited in 1903, is one of the most comprehensive books on the early days of the Cat Fancy that has ever been written. It has been published worldwide and is a never-ending source of interest. Every breed is described, some illustrated in colour; there are photographs of owners and their catteries, anecdotes about their cats, their show successes and personal reminiscences. Cat Clubs and their officers and committees, cats and catteries in America, advice on rearing kittens, colour breeding and cat management, cat shows and how to enter them, in fact everything one could wish to know, is all set down in a personal, interesting way.

Miss Simpson followed this with a small handbook, entitled *Cats and All About Them*. She refers to this book as 'her little yellow book'. Later the title was changed to *Cats for Pleasure and Profit*! It is full of charming hints on care and management of cats – 'Don't have anything to do with red baize or flannel in making a bed for young kittens. If these materials get wet the dye comes out and stains the coats horribly. The other day I came across a little family of Blues with red tails.'

There are anthologies, such as the well-known *A Dictionary of Cat Lovers* by Lady Aberconway, a most comprehensive volume containing excerpts from the works of almost every writer from the fifteenth century BC to the twentieth century AD, arranged alphabetically according to the name of the person; the pages of acknowledgements are daunting. This is a stupendous collection of writings and pictures, and a never-ending source of interest and reference. Published by Michael Joseph in 1949, it is a book that all cat-lovers will want to possess.

Driver : Anyway, there'll be a drink for us at the end of this trip!

The Christmas party.

Cartoons by Louis Wain which appeared in *Our Cats* in December 1961.

Carl van Vechten's *The Tiger in the House*, published by Heinemann in 1921, is another such book. 'The Cat in Folklore', 'The Cat and the Law', 'The Cat in the Theatre' and 'The Cat in Music' are some of the chapter headings, with the author's own ideas and comments. It is a book to return to time and time again.

A book with a show flavour, with full colour photographs by Sally Anne Thompson, is *Champion Cats of the World* by Ing and Pond, with 96 photographs of the world's most beautiful pedigree cats. Many books speak briefly about shows but there are very few with so many names of owners and breeders of show cats, with photographs and names of the actual cats, as Mrs May Eustace's *The World of Show Cats* published in 1970 by Pelham Books Limited. Winning cats in all breeds in various parts of the world are mentioned and over a hundred are photographed.

It is time here to write a little of Louis Wain as not only was he involved in the Cat Fancy almost from the beginning, being a cat judge, Chairman and show manager of the National Cat Club, but his books at that time must have been among the best-sellers. Every year annuals appeared with his amusing drawings showing cats behaving as human beings, playing golf, football, attending parties and school. His drawings now are in much demand and fetch high prices.

STAMPS

Several countries have issued stamps with cats on. There is a 13-cent USA stamp depicting an American Cocker Spaniel with a grey cat behind it. Thailand has issued a very attractive stamp featuring an all-grey shorthair cat of foreign type, perhaps a Korat, although the caption says 'Siamese Cat. Blue Point.' Poland has had two issues of cat stamps, and in 1966 Luxembourg pictured the witch's cat. Spain tucked Lindbergh's black cat into the lower right-hand corner of a stamp in their issue commemorating famous aviators. Lindbergh left his cat at home because he did not wish to risk its life as well as his own. There is a Turkish stamp featuring a big white Angora. Hungary, Vietnam, Equatorial Guinea, Bahrain and Paraguay have all depicted cats on stamp issues. The Kingdom of Yemen has issued a very spectacular large stamp picturing a Siamese cat. Siamese kittens appear on a stamp issued by the United Emirates.

One must search hard to find the cat between the chimneys in the 16p Christmas stamp issued in 1983 by the Post Office in Great Britain, but there it is, a black and white magpie cat with a white tip to its tail, with the three Kings of Orient as chimneys and a white dove of peace.

10 Cat Clubs and the Cat Fancy

The word 'Fancy' seems to puzzle and also amuse some people, but the term has been used for many, many years in connection with the breeding of animals such as mice and rabbits as well as cats. The dictionary defines 'fancy' as 'to breed or cultivate, with a view to development of conventionally accepted points.' The word came officially into the cat world with the formation of the Governing Council of the Cat Fancy (GCCF) in 1910, and is very much used still. In 1876 Dr Gordon Stables, a writer and early judge of cats, said at the time of writing *The Domestic Cat*, which was a small handbook compared with a larger one he had written two or three years previously, 'that now Cats, indeed, have become quite a "fancy", and much greater pains are now taken to try to breed pussy up to as nearly a standard of perfection as possible.' He went on to say that cat shows too have become much more numerous all over the country. It is difficult to find out much about these early shows and who organised them, apart from those held at the Crystal Palace.

Chas Ross in his *Book of Cats* published in 1868, before the first cat show, gave quite explicit details of certain kinds of cats, saying that the domestic species required no description, but that 'the Cat of Angora is a very beautiful variety, with silvery hair of fine silken texture, generally longest on the neck, but also long on the tail. Some are yellowish, and others olive, approaching the colour of the Lion.' He said that 'this breed of Cats has singular taste', and he knew one that took kindly to gin and water, and was rather partial to curry. He continued: 'The Persian Cat is a variety with hair very long and very silky, perhaps more so than the Cat of Angora; it is however differently coloured, being of a fine uniform grey on the upper part, with the texture of the fur as soft as silk, and the lustre glossy; the colour fades off on the lower parts of the sides and passes into white, or nearly so, on the belly. This is, probably, one of the most beautiful varieties, and it is said to be exceedingly gentle in its manner.'

He wrote too about the 'Chinese Cat' whose origin it is difficult to trace. The description he gave was that this cat 'has the fur beautifully glossed, but it is very different from either of those which have been mentioned. It is variegated with black and yellow, and unlike most of the race, has the ears pendulous.' He went on to say that 'Bosman, writing about the ears, says "It is worthy of observation, that there is in animals evident signs of ancestry of their slavery. Long ears are produced by time and civilisation, and all wild animals have straight round ears."' Today, cats known as Fold-ears, i.e. with ears that are bent down but in no way can be called pendulous, have been bred in Great Britain. They are not recognised in Britain, as the Royal Veterinary College here were not happy about certain aspects that may occur in breeding. They are recognised in the United States. The puzzle remains as to whether the cats did actually come from China and what happened to them eventually.

Chas Ross referred to the Tortoiseshell or Spanish Cat as 'one of the prettiest varieties of those which have the fur of moderate length, and without any particular silvery gloss. The colours are very pure, black, white and reddish orange, and in this country, at least, males thus marked are said to be very rare, though they are quite common in Egypt and the south of Europe.' They would be known as Tortoiseshell and White today, and occasional males are born, but are usually found to be infertile.

He was very uncomplimentary about the

Manx Cat, saying 'It is the most singular; its limbs are gaunt; its fur close set, its eyes staring and restless, and it has no tail, that is to say, there is only a sort of knob as thought its tail had been amputated. He quoted another writer as saying 'A black Manx cat with its staring eyes and its stump of a tail, is a most measly looking beast . . . . It might be fitly the quadrupedal form in which the ancient sorcerers were wont to clothe themselves on nocturnal excursions.' Very few Manx are seen at the British shows today, but they are very popular in the States, where there is also a longhaired variety. It may be possible to order direct from the Isle of Man, from where they are said to have originated, but I believe they have a long waiting list. Today's Manx must have no trace of a tail, and if having the start of one would be known as a Stumpy, and not really a true Manx.

The first dog show was held in Britain in 1859, with the Kennel Club being founded in 1873, so in all probability the schedules for the first cat show were similar to those of the dog shows, and the aims and purposes of the National Cat Club as a registering body also similar to those of the Kennel Club.

As fanciers became interested in specific varieties, they were anxious to meet fellow breeders to discuss any problems that may arise and to learn how to improve their particular stock. Thus the first breed clubs came into being, that is clubs interested in definite varieties as apart from the regional all-breed clubs which catered for all varieties.

Clubs are the backbone of the Cat Fancy. Without them there would be no GCCF, as it is the members of the various affiliated clubs that elect a delegate or delegates according to the number of their membership, i.e. if less than 200, a club is allowed one delegate and, if over 200, two. Clubs that have less than 100 members, unless one of the founder clubs, do not quality for a delegate. A new club has to be in being for a number of years before it can be affiliated to the GCCF.

The Council holds a meeting each quarter which the delegates from the clubs have to attend, and this could mean over 140 delegates taking part. The delegates are elected by the member at the Annual General Meetings of the affiliated clubs. They attend their first meeting in June, which is referred to as the Electoral Meeting, as the officers and members of the various committees are elected for the coming year. There are six such committees, the Executive, Finance, Disciplinary, Investigation, Appeals, Cat Care and a Genetics Committee, all of which are necessary for the day-to-day running of the Cat Fancy.

Up to now the Council's main work, that of registering and transferring to new owners cats and kittens, has been dealt with by the Registrars (the Longhair, the Shorthair, the Burmese and the Siamese), all working from their own homes. The work has grown so much over the years, as pedigree cats and kittens have increased in number, that the GCCF decided it was necessary to have an official headquarters. 1983 saw the establishment of such offices in Bridgewater, Somerset, where most of the work is to be carried out. A computer has been installed which is speeding up the Council's work.

One aspect of the work is the granting of prefixes. A prefix is a cattery name for which a fee is charged, but which is the sole use of a particular breeder and can only be used for registering kittens of his or her breeding. It appears on the pedigree before the name actually given to the animal. Over 1,000 are granted each year.

The Council approves standards of points for new varieties, and issues a booklet giving full details of all the recognised varieties and the points allocated for the specific characteristics required. It published show rules, lists of cat shows, and from time to time a stud book. It approves the names of new judges put forward by the various panels of clubs.

Over 70 shows a year are run under the sponsorship of the Council. This includes about 50 Championship Shows at which challenge certificates are given to the winners of the open breed class, should they be up to the required standard, and similarly premier certificates to the neuter cats. By winning three challenge certificates at three separate shows under three different judges a cat can become a Champion and may then compete in the Champion of Champions classes, and under similar conditions become a Grand Champion. Similarly a neuter can become a Premier, and then a Grand Premier, all subject to the approval of the Council.

The Council grants permission for Sanction Shows to be held. These are really rehearsals by clubs for Championship Shows, which are only permitted when a club has run a number of Sanction and Exemption Shows. Challenge certificates are not given at Sanction Shows, nor are they at Exemption Shows. The latter are held under similar rules to other shows, but the classes are not necessarily divided into male and female, and the number of classes offered may be comparatively small. They give an opportunity for novices to show their stock and to get the opinion of well-known judges as to a kitten's potentialities. They also teach novice exhibitors show procedure.

Many of the shows put on pet cat classes if they have sufficient room. These classes encourage the owners to look after their pets, and many eventually become interested in pedigree breeding, or owning and showing a neutered pedigree pet. There are now classes at some shows for kittens or cats with one pedigree parent and one unknown parent. They cannot compete for championships.

The All-breed Clubs have been responsible over the years for welcoming fanciers interested in all varieties or a specific variety, and most run shows for all varieties. The Breed Clubs, of which there are more than 40, look after the interests of specific breeders. Over the years they have been responsible for agreeing standards, altering and amending them if thought necessary, and then seeking the Council's approval. They help experimental breeders endeavouring to produce new colours and types of cats by advising and putting them in touch with others equally interested. The GCCF publishes a list of clubs annually, with up-to-date addresses of secretaries at a cost of £1 plus a stamped addressed envelope.

Most Breed Clubs organise shows for their particular variety or varieties, with the Siamese having several breed clubs, some for cats and kittens with specific coloured points, and the Siamese Cat Club for all varieties of Siamese. The Longhaired Cat Club runs a show for all longhairs, and the Blue Persian runs one for Blue Persians. All-breed shows put on classes for all varieties, and if large enough may be divided into separate sections, i.e. Longhair, Shorthair, British and Foreign Shorthair, and Siamese. To cut down the rising costs some of the smaller breed clubs are running their shows jointly with another breed club, i.e. the Blue Persian with the White Persian Club.

All-breed and Breed Club Shows are held all over the British Isles, including Northern Ireland, Scotland, Wales, the Channel Islands, and many towns in England, such as London, Birmingham, Crawley, Southampton, Newton Abbott, Bournemouth and others. It is difficult to find suitable halls in London nowadays, but the Kensington Kitten and Neuter Cat Club holds a show in Westminster in July, and the National Cat Club organises a very large show with over 2,000 exhibits at Olympia, London, in early December. Smaller shows are held frequently in the suburbs, with the leisure centres being much favoured. In fact, on most Saturdays throughout the year, there is probably a cat show being held somewhere in the country, even several on the same day. The GCCF publish an annual list of shows taking place throughout the year. The cost is £1 plus a stamped addressed envelope.

It is not necessary to belong to a club to exhibit at shows, but there are advantages in doing so. Being a member of the club running the show may mean reduced prices for the classes entered, and gives the opportunity of winning cups and the special prizes offered for members only. Belonging to a club does mean meeting fellow breeders and cat lovers at the Annual General Meetings, and possibly social events put on by some clubs for members during the year. Many a lonely person has made lifelong friends through the Cat Fancy.

One can become a breeder without belonging to a cat club or registering with the GCCF, but anyone going in for breeding would certainly do better selling certified pedigree stock, and could also show, and by winning enhance the value. Unfortunately there are a number of back-street breeders who look on cats as mere machines, producing as many kittens as possible, caring little to whom they are sold, and failing to give the correct feeding and attention necessary to produce really strong healthy kittens. The unfortunate buyer of these is invariably in for trouble. Some clubs keep a list of kittens for sale bred by their members which they can recommend.

Appendix: The Breed Numbers

Longhaired

1	Black
1	White (Blue-eyed)
2a	White (Orange-eyed)
2b	White (Odd-eyed)
3	Blue
4	Red Self
5	Cream
6	Smoke
6a	Blue Smoke
7	Silver Tabby
8	Brown Tabby
9	Red Tabby
10	Chinchilla
11	Tortoiseshell
12	Tortoiseshell and White
12a	Bi-coloured
13	Blue-cream
13a	Any Other Colour
13b	(1) Seal Colourpoint
13b	(2) Blue Colourpoint
13b	(3) Chocolate Colourpoint
13b	(4) Lilac Colourpoint
13b	(5) Red Colourpoint
13b	(6) Tortie Colourpoint
13b	(7) Cream Colourpoint
13b	(8) Blue-cream Colourpoint
13b	(9) Choc. Tortie Colourpoint
13b	(10) Lilac Cream Colourpoint
13b	(11) Tabby Point Seal Colourpoint
13b	(12) Tabby Point Blue C.P.
13b	13 Tabby Point Chocolate C.P.
13b	14 Tabby Point Lilac C.P.
13b	15 Tabby Point Red C.P.
13b	16 Tabby Point Tortie C.P.
13b	17 Tabby Point Cream C.P.
13b	18 Tabby Point Blue/Cream C.P.
13b	19 Tabby Point Choc/Tortie C.P.
13b	20 Tabby Point Lilac/Cream C.P.
13c	Birman
13d	Turkish

50b	Self Chocolate
50c	Self Lilac
51	(1) Red Shell Cameo
51	(2) Red Shaded Cameo
51	(3) Red Smoke Cameo
51	(4) Red Tortie Cameo
52	(1) Cream Shell Cameo
52	(2) Cream Shaded Cameo
52	(3) Cream Smoke Cameo
52	(4) Blue/Cream Cameo
53	Pewter

Shorthaired

14	White (Blue-eyed)
14a	White (Orange-eyed)
14b	White (Odd-eyed)
15	Black
16	British Blue
16a	Russian Blue
17	Cream
18	Silver Tabby
19	Red Tabby
20	Brown Tabby
21	Tortoiseshell
22	Tortoiseshell and White
23	Abyssinian
23a	Sorrel Abyssinian
23c	Blue Abyssinian
25	Manx
25a	Stumpie Manx
25b	Tailed Manx
27	Brown Burmese
27a	Blue Burmese
27b	Chocolate Burmese
27c	Lilac Burmese
27d	Red Burmese
27e	Brown Tortie Burmese
27f	Cream Burmese
27g	Blue Tortie Burmese
27h	Choc. Tortie Burmese
27j	Lilac Tortie Burmese
28	Blue-cream
29	Havana
29c	Foreign Lilac

30	Spotted
31	Bi-coloured
33	Cornish Rex
33a	Devon Rex
34	Korat
35	Foreign White
36	Smoke
37	Foreign Black
37a	Foreign Blue
38	Brown Oriental Spotted Tabby
38a	Blue Oriental Spotted Tabby
38b	Chocolate Oriental Spotted Tabby
38c	Lilac Oriental Spotted Tabby
38d	Red Oriental Spotted Tabby
38f	Cream Oriental Spotted Tabby
39	British Shorthair Tipped

Siamese

24	**Sealpoint Siamese**
24a	**Bluepoint Siamese**
24b	**Chocpoint Siamese**
24c	**Lilacpoint Siamese**
32	**Tabbypoint Siamese**
32a	**Redpoint Siamese**
32b	**Tortiepoint Siamese**
32c	**Creampoint Siamese**

Balinese

61	Sealpoint
61a	Bluepoint
61b	Chocolatepoint
61c	Lilacpoint
61d	Redpoint
61e	Seal Tortiepoint
61f	Creampoint
61g	Blue Tortiepoint
61h	Chocolate Tortiepoint
61j	Lilac Tortiepoint

Plus t for Tabby, v for Variant

Index